VALUE-FOR-MONEY AUDIT EVIDENCE

OTHER STUDIES IN THIS SERIES

Use and Meaning of "Market" in Inventory Valuation
Overhead as an Element of Inventory Costs
Canadian University Accounting
Accounting for Trust and Loan Companies in Canada
Translation of Foreign Currencies
Earnings Forecasts
Capital Budgeting Practices Including the Impact of Inflation
Extent of Audit Testing
Limited Audit Engagements and the Expression of Negative Assurance
Corporate Reporting: Its Future Evolution
Accounting for Pension Costs and Liabilities
Audit Committees
Analytical Review
Financial Reporting for Credit Unions
Accounting for Portfolio Investments
Financial Statements for Pension Plan Participants
Pension Plan Auditing
Materiality — the Concept and its Application to Auditing
Local Government Financial Reporting
Accounting and Financial Reporting by Agricultural Producers
Accounting and Financial Reporting by Venture Capital Organizations
Accounting and Financial Reporting by Junior Mining Companies
Professional Judgment in Financial Reporting
Incorporating the Time Value of Money Within Financial Accounting
Accounting and Reporting for Physical Assets by Governments
The Financial Statement Presentation of Corporate Financing Activities
Information to be Included in the Annual Report to Shareholders

VALUE-FOR-MONEY AUDIT EVIDENCE

D.M. Barnes, CA

The Canadian Institute of Chartered Accountants

A RESEARCH STUDY

This Study is one of a series commissioned by the Studies and Standards Department as part of the CICA's continuing research program. Each Study in this series expresses the views of the author or Study Group concerned, but have not been adopted, endorsed, approved, disapproved or otherwise acted upon by a Committee, the governing body or membership of the CICA or any provincial Institute/Ordre.

These Studies are intended to stimulate thought, discussion and debate on matters of accounting and auditing theory and practice. The Studies and Standards Department earnestly solicits comments from readers on the matters dealt with in this Study.

Canadian Cataloguing in Publication Data

Barnes, D. M.
Value-for-money audit evidence

D.M. Barnes, principal author and chair of study group.
Includes bibliographical references.
ISBN 0-88800-261-0

1. Auditing. 2. Evidence. I. Canadian Institute of Chartered Accountants. II. Title.

HF5667.B37 1991 657'.45 C92-093312-2

Printed in Canada
Disponible en français
ISBN 0-88800-261-0

FOREWORD

The process of gathering and evaluating evidence is fundamental to an audit engagement. The rigour with which these tasks are performed helps to distinguish auditing from other types of engagements. Public Sector Auditing Statement 4, Value-for-Money Auditing Standards, issued by the Public Sector Accounting and Auditing Committee in March 1988, states that, "Sufficient appropriate audit evidence should be obtained to afford a reasonable basis to support the content of the auditor's report.". The exercise of professional judgment underlies the auditor's evaluation of when that standard is met in a value-for-money audit engagement. Nevertheless, guidance based upon sound accepted practices can be provided to assist auditors.

The types and sources of audit evidence in a value-for-money audit may vary in emphasis as compared to financial statement audits. For example, auditors may rely more heavily on such techniques as enquiry and discussion when conducting a value-for-money audit. Value-for-money audit evidence tends to be more subjective and it is not clear how auditors apply professional judgment in determining the sufficiency and appropriateness of evidence.

Value-for-money audit mandates have different reporting requirements. In many mandates, auditors report directly on the performance of an entity, either by identifying deficiencies or by providing an overall opinion. In other mandates, auditors may attest to management representations. There has been debate as to the nature and extent of evidence required to support the auditor's conclusions under each of these reporting frameworks.

There has been considerable study within the CICA and by other professional bodies of audit evidence in the context of the audit of financial statements. Little guidance exists, however, for interpreting and applying the standard on evidence set out in Public Sector Auditing Statement 4 in value-for-money audits. In April 1990, the Public Sector Accounting and Auditing Committee decided that a Research Study should be commissioned to consider the concept of audit evidence and its applicability to value-for-money audit evidence. D.M. Barnes, CA, of Peat Marwick Thorne, a member of PSAAC, agreed to be the principal author of the Study and to chair a Study Group that would consider the issues of relevance to the subject.

The Terms of Reference for the principal author and the Study Group were to:

1. conduct research and provide background information on audit evidence in value-for-money auditing by reviewing relevant literature and current practice.
2. discuss the concept of evidence in auditing, including the legal dimension of evidence, and assess its applicability to value-for-money auditing.
3. identify and discuss the key areas where professional judgment needs to be exercised in performing value-for-money audits (for example, planning decisions regarding objectives, scope and criteria; examination decisions, such as identifying exceptions; and reporting decisions, such as determining what to report) and their impact on the necessary audit evidence.
4. identify, describe and assess:
    - the relative reliability of the various types and sources of audit evidence that can be used in performing value-for-money audits, and
    - the appropriateness of the methods used for gathering evidence in value-for-money audits.
5. identify, describe and assess the appropriateness of current practices used to evaluate audit evidence in value-for-money audits (including examples of current practice regarding evidence for value-for-money audits having different objectives and scope).
6. determine whether the factors for evaluating audit evidence vary depending on the stage of the audit (planning, examination and reporting) and on the reporting requirements and assess the impact of such differences.
7. contrast practices commonly used in financial statement audits with value-for-money audit practices.
8. provide conclusions as to possible preferred practices related to value-for-money auditing, including:
    - the nature and sources of evidence;
    - methods for gathering evidence; and
    - evaluating evidence.

The primary purpose of the Study is to stimulate discussion and debate on this important topic. The Study Group acknowledges that further research will be required to fully accomplish the terms of reference set out above, due to the fact that the subject of value-for-money auditing is in the developing stage, and there are still a number of gaps in theory and many differences in practice.

The Studies and Standards Department expresses its appreciation to D.M. Barnes, CA, for the time and effort spent in preparing the Study, and to the members of the Study Group for their interest in the project and the contributions made. Thanks are also expressed to J. Ralston, CA, of the Office of the Auditor General in Ottawa, for the research assistance to the author and the Study Group, and to Donald E. Sheehy, CA, Senior Manager, Research Studies, for administering the project.

Toronto
November 1991

David J. Moore, CA
Research Studies Director

STUDY GROUP

D.M. Barnes, CA
Principal Author & Chairman
Ottawa, Ontario

G. Bédard, FCGA
Bureau de Vérificateur général du Québec
Québec, Québec

B.S. Caine, FCA
Ernst & Young
Toronto, Ontario

J.P. Gregory, CA
Office of the Auditor General of British Columbia
Victoria, B.C.

B.P. Miller, CA
Office of the Auditor General of Canada
Ottawa, Ontario

R. Palmer, CA
Regional Municipality of Ottawa-Carleton
Ottawa, Ontario

A.J.K. Wingate, CA
Office of the Auditor General of Alberta
Edmonton, Alberta

TABLE OF CONTENTS

OVERVIEW

A very significant part of a value-for-money audit is devoted to gathering evidence to confirm facts that in turn provide evidence to support audit findings and conclusions. During the audit examination, interviews are conducted, work sites are visited, reports are reviewed and systems are evaluated. The information obtained is often fragmented and difficult to fit into easily understood patterns. As the audit progresses, the facts that have been gathered are compared with the detailed criteria (or expected standards of performance), allowing the auditor to reach a number of preliminary judgments, or findings. The auditor uses these findings to conclude whether the audit objectives and criteria have been met. 1

In a value-for-money audit, it is usually possible to establish a great many facts about a wide range of activities and functions, all within the scope of the audit. The techniques used to gather evidence are usually readily understood by those conducting the audit. What is much more difficult to determine, however, is how much and what kind of evidence is needed, and what type of analysis is appropriate after the evidence has been gathered. 2

The focus in this study has been on providing answers to these questions, to the extent that this is possible, and on exploring basic concepts so that the process of gathering and evaluating evidence can be better understood. 3

The search for underlying concepts has taken two main directions: 4

- This study identifies the items in the auditor's report requiring audit evidence, including objectives, scope, criteria, facts, findings, conclusions and recommendations. It then assesses the factors that determine the evidence needed to support each of these items in the report.
- Having established a framework for reviewing value-for-money audit evidence, this study turns to concepts that might be helpful in assessing what constitutes *sufficient appropriate audit evidence*, so that the nature and extent of evidence required to support items in the report can be determined. The relevance of financial statement and legal evidence concepts is assessed and, although useful parallels with value-for-money evidence are identified, the primary concepts associated with these forms of evidence are deemed not to be appropriate for adoption by value-for-money auditors. This study then traces auditing to its roots,

to logic concepts and the process of reasoning. Logic models are used to help understand the nature of value-for-money audit evidence. The concept of persuasive evidence is examined and found to be important in describing the degree of support required for audit findings and conclusions — in other words, sufficient appropriate audit evidence.

5 This approach parallels legal concepts of evaluating evidence. Juries, for example, do not rate the cases presented to them by the prosecution and defence as an 8 out of 10 or some similar measure of probability. Instead, they use judgment, based on the evidence presented to them, to reach a verdict. Similarly, in a value-for-money audit, the auditor's professional judgment must predominate in an assessment of the sufficiency and appropriateness of audit evidence.

6 Building on concepts deemed to be appropriate for value-for-money audits, the study considers four basic types of evidence: physical, documentary, oral and analytical. The importance of interviews as a source of evidence in a value-for-money audit is stressed, together with the need for corroborating evidence.

7 Perhaps the most critical stage in a value-for-money audit is the point at which evidence is evaluated to establish audit findings and conclusions. The study proposes approaches to evaluating evidence, and lists specific factors to be considered by the auditor in carrying out this evaluation.

8 The study assesses the impact of different audit mandates on the nature and extent of evidence required. Mandates within Canada, including special examinations, and mandates in several other countries are included in this assessment.

9 The study also analyzes the results of a survey of current practices, and comments on the views and preferred practices of the respondents. The responses to this survey raise several issues that the Study Group believes require careful consideration by practitioners.

10 Practitioners face a number of challenges related to value-for-money audit evidence. Standards and guidelines are needed to assist practitioners in evaluating sufficient appropriate audit evidence. Before these are developed, however, sufficient time should be allowed for practitioners to discuss and experiment with the ideas put forward in this study.

11 The Study Group believes that specific guidance by the Public Sector Accounting and Auditing Committee is needed on:

- interpreting the term *sufficient appropriate audit evidence*;
- applying risk and significance concepts to value-for-money auditing; and
- suggesting appropriate techniques for obtaining and evaluating evidence.

Chapter 1

INTRODUCTION

BACKGROUND TO THE STUDY

Value-for-money (VFM) auditing in Canada has had a relatively short history. Beginning with new value-for-money mandates given to several public sector auditors in the late 1970s, practice has evolved steadily as new mandates have been created and new approaches have been introduced. The formation of the Canadian Comprehensive Auditing Foundation in 1980 has also provided a focal point for research and development. 1

VFM auditing focuses on the economical and efficient management of public funds and resources, and on the effectiveness of programs. VFM audits are conducted in a complex environment, characterized by continuous change. Planning, conducting and reporting these audits present an ongoing challenge to the auditor. 2

In recent years, as practice has expanded and matured, there has been increasing emphasis on reviewing the basic concepts underlying VFM auditing. Differences in practice that have emerged are being assessed and practitioners are increasingly engaged in discussion and debate about ways to benefit from past experience. 3

This examination of underlying concepts has been given added impetus by the CICA's Public Sector Accounting and Auditing Committee (PSAAC). In March 1988, PSAAC released Public Sector Auditing Statement 4, *Value-for-Money Auditing Standards*, that includes general, examination and reporting standards. 4

To assist practitioners in understanding and applying the standards, PSAAC issued Public Sector Auditing Guidelines on *Planning Value-for-Money Audits* in March 1990 and on *Knowledge of the Audit Entity in Planning Value-for-Money Audits* in November 1990 VFM audit evidence is another area in which PSAAC identified the need for guidance. Before proceeding, however, PSAAC determined that research was needed before guidelines or standards could be developed. 5

Why should evidence be identified as a subject for research? One compelling reason is that evidence is basic to auditing. Consider, for example, a definition of auditing that is widely accepted in both Canada and the United States, contained in 6 an American Accounting Association research study, *A Statement of Basic Auditing Concepts*:

> ...a systematic process of objectively obtaining and evaluating evidence regarding assertions about economic actions and events to ascertain the degree of correspondence between those assertions and established criteria and communicating the results to interested users.[1]

7 This definition gives two clear messages: evidence is at the heart of the audit process, and both obtaining and evaluating evidence are essential parts of that process. In commenting on the concept of evidence, the study concludes that:

> Objectively obtaining and evaluating evidence is the essence of auditing...all audits center on the process of obtaining and evaluating evidence.[2]

8 While the need for evidence to support VFM audit conclusions has always been recognized, there is less certainty about the nature and extent of that evidence. Ideally, auditors would like to have as much evidence as possible to back up their conclusions. On the other hand, there are limitations in time, staff and dollars that force auditors to make choices as to the type and amount of evidence they can gather.

9 Since a major part of most audits is devoted to gathering and evaluating evidence, decisions on evidence are clearly important ones. But how can a research study on evidence help the auditor in making these decisions?

10 To answer this question, it is necessary to consider the essential nature of VFM auditing. This form of auditing has developed in the public sector with quite different objectives from financial statement auditing. Certainly the types of audit reports that have evolved are fundamentally different from those traditionally associated with the audit of financial statements. To date, however, most of the Canadian literature about audit evidence deals with financial statement audit evidence.

11 As Anderson observed rather prophetically in *The External Audit*:

> As it is socially useful at the present time to provide attestation to historically based financial statements, GAAS [generally accepted auditing standards] embody this objective in their reporting and examination standards. Auditing theory must therefore provide a logical method for complying with these standards. In the future, should it become socially useful to meet some additional or alternative objectives (whether reporting on forecasts, internal control, management performance, or otherwise), such objectives will no doubt be incorporated in a revised set of GAAS. Auditing theory will then have to develop an appropriate approach to meeting those revised standards.[3]

12 There are now VFM auditing standards; it is time to consider their impact on traditional auditing theory and concepts. This research study addresses the fundamental nature of audit evidence, examines underlying concepts and assesses the application of these concepts to existing VFM audit practices.

---

1 American Accounting Association, *A Statement of Basic Auditing Concepts*, Studies in Accounting Research #6, 1973, p. 2.

2 *Ibid.*, p. 2.

3 Anderson, R.J., *The External Audit*, Second Edition, Copp Clark Pitman, 1984, p. 139.

STUDY OBJECTIVES, APPROACH AND SCOPE

PSAAC has provided the following statement of purpose for this research study: 13

> The objective of the project is to study the concept of audit evidence and practice for obtaining and assessing it in value-for-money auditing. Auditors are concerned with audit evidence in all phases of a value-for-money audit. Professional judgment is required by the auditor in determining the nature and extent of the audit evidence required in each phase.

There are two main sources of the information on which the study's observations and conclusions are based: 14

- a review of relevant Canadian and international literature on audit evidence, and literature on legal evidence, logic and reasoning, professional judgment, and other related areas. (A more detailed description of the literature review is contained in Appendix A.)
- a survey of current practice through mailing 75 questionnaires to a wide cross-section of practitioners across Canada, and an analysis of the responses. (A copy of the survey questionnaire is included as Appendix B.)

The literature review and survey of practice were supplemented by interviews with individuals representing different areas of expertise related to evidence. 15

To meet the objectives of the study, basic auditing theory and underlying concepts of evidence were examined as well as existing practices. Building on these evidence concepts, the study explains how they might be applied to different VFM mandates, including those of federal and provincial legislative auditors, special examiners, municipal auditors, internal auditors and other VFM practitioners. It also discusses the types and sources of VFM audit evidence and methods of gathering and evaluating that evidence. 16

Although this study deals primarily with external rather than internal auditing, most of the material in the study should be of interest to internal auditors. In gathering information for this study, therefore, the views of internal auditors were sought through a review of internal audit literature and by including internal auditors in the survey of current practice. 17

FOCUS OF THE STUDY

Although a considerable amount of research has been carried out on concepts of audit evidence as they relate to the audit of financial statements, very little has been written on VFM audit evidence concepts. A discussion paper written by Maier Zelman in 1980 speculated on the basic nature of the evidence gathered in value-for-money 18 audits,[4] but subsequent literature has dealt primarily with the types of VFM audit evidence and how evidence is gathered and evaluated.

19 The scarcity of research is not entirely unexpected. For example, the research study that is widely regarded as the pioneer work on auditing theory is Mautz and Sharaf's *The Philosophy of Auditing*.[5] Commenting on the absence of literature on auditing concepts at the time their study was published in 1961, Mautz and Sharaf observed:

> We have a strong tendency in auditing to adopt a pragmatic approach. Whatever works well is adopted and strongly advocated; what has not yet been found applicable has little appeal. ...We must continually test our practices and procedures, not only in actual practice, but against the theory which underlies auditing.[6]

20 During the relatively brief history of VFM auditing, VFM auditors have been similarly occupied with interpreting and applying the mandates given to them. As a result, there has been relatively little exploration to date of underlying concepts.

21 A successful study of VFM audit evidence depends upon an understanding of the underlying concepts of evidence. A conceptual framework is important because it provides a basis for interpreting terms such as "sufficient" and "appropriate" audit evidence. This study, therefore, addresses basic VFM audit evidence concepts; in doing so, it attempts to place VFM auditing in the wider context of auditing theory.

22 A second, equally important focal point of the study is the application of these concepts to VFM audit practice. Having a theoretical framework for VFM audit evidence is important, but it is also necessary to show that the theories have practical application. The survey responses received as part of this study provide a snapshot of current practices and attitudes. They represent, perhaps for the first time, a comprehensive view of what practitioners think about VFM audit evidence. These views have been carefully considered in assessing the practicality of the various conceptual approaches explored during the study.

23 Since this is new territory, this study suggests approaches that may vary from those now in use. By stimulating discussion and experimentation, however, the Study Group hopes to contribute to the continuing development of VFM auditing principles and practice.

---

4 Zelman, Maier, *Evidence in Value-for-Money Auditing*, Discussion Paper No. 2, Office of the Auditor General of Canada, January 1980. This Discussion Paper looked at parallels between legal and value-for-money audit evidence and concluded that:

"...the standards of evidence for the management auditor should perhaps be the civil law approach of the plaintiff's advocate. This means that the auditor must be reasonably certain that there is a probability of there being a case, subject to preponderance of the evidence. Adequate evidence in this case would be what a 'reasonable man' would accept as being grounds for belief." [p. 8].

5 Mautz, R.K., Sharaf, H.A., *The Philosophy of Auditing*, American Accounting Association Monograph No. 6, 1961.

6 *Ibid.*, p.17.

Chapter 2

DEFINITIONS AND STANDARDS

INTRODUCTION

Most of the terms used in this study are familiar ones, but some mean different things to different people. Some are common to the practice of law and also to the study of logic. Terms that will play an essential part in the discussions in this and later chapters include *evidence, facts, findings and conclusions.* To avoid a misunderstanding as to the intended meaning of these and other terms, various dictionary and other definitions are provided, followed by the meanings used for the purposes of this study. 1

PSAAC Statements and Guidelines include many references to audit evidence. These standards and guidelines will be referred to frequently in this study, since they provide the framework within which VFM audit practice is conducted. Standards and guidance related to financial statement audits are also of considerable interest, since practice in this area is well-established. The section of the CICA *Handbook* on audit evidence is particularly relevant. 2

PSAAC Statements and Guidelines related to evidence are presented in Appendix C. Section 5300 of the CICA *Handbook*, Audit Evidence, is included in Appendix D. 3

DEFINITIONS OF EVIDENCE

A logical place to begin a discussion of value-for-money audit evidence is to decide what is meant by "evidence". Some of the definitions in dictionaries and other reference sources describe everyday usages of the term evidence. Others provide definitions of legal or audit evidence. Definitions of evidence include: 4

> that which tends to prove or disprove something; ground for belief; proof.[1]
>
> testimony, facts, in support *of* [or *for*] a conclusion.[2]

---

1 *Random House Dictionary of the English Language*, Unabridged, Second Edition, 1987.

2 *Concise Oxford Dictionary of Current English*, Seventh Edition, Oxford University Press, 1982.

5 Legal evidence is defined as:

> data presented to a court or jury in proof of the facts in issue and which may include the testimony of witnesses, records, documents, or objects.[3]

> something that furnishes or tends to furnish proof...; something legally submitted to a competent tribunal as a means of ascertaining the truth of any alleged matter of fact under investigation before it.[4]

6 Reference sources on the accounting and auditing use of the term evidence include:

> A collection of *facts*, admittedly or allegedly accurate, relevant, and sufficient, offered in verification of a *proposition*. Its recognition and admissibility are established under rules laid down by courts, learned professions, and other institutions. Evidence differs from belief, which may not be supported by acceptable evidence.[5]

> The data and information an auditor obtains during audit field work to document findings and support opinions and conclusions.[6]

7 Two themes run through all of these definitions: evidence as *something that furnishes proof* and evidence as *support for conclusions*. These themes will be considered in depth in subsequent chapters.

STANDARDS

8 One of the examination standards included in PSAAC's *Value-for-Money Auditing Standards* states that:

> Sufficient appropriate audit evidence should be obtained to afford a reasonable basis to support the content of the auditor's report.[7]

This evidence standard will form the basis for much of the discussion of VFM audit evidence.

9 A similar evidence standard exists for financial statement audits. Section 5100 of the CICA *Handbook* contains the following examination standard:

> Sufficient appropriate audit evidence should be obtained, by such means as inspection, observation, enquiry, confirmation, computation and analysis, to afford a reasonable basis to support the content of the report.

10 As is immediately apparent, the only differences between the VFM and financial statement standards are the inclusion of the means of obtaining evidence, which are listed in the financial statement standard but not the VFM standard, and the addition of the word "auditor's" before "report" in the VFM standard.

---

3 Random House Dictionary.

4 *Websters Third New International Dictionary*, Unabridged.

5 *Kohler's Dictionary for Accountants*, 6th Edition, Prentice-Hall Inc., 1983.

6 United States General Accounting Office *Government Auditing Standards*, 1988 Revision, p. G-3.

7 CICA Public Sector Auditing Statement 4, *Value-for-Money Auditing Standards*, para. .31.

The Study Group interprets this latter addition to be one of clarification only. In both standards, the report referred to is that presented by the auditor on completion of the audit examination. Although other reports may be produced by a VFM auditor in the course of the audit, for example, a survey report at the end of the planning phase, the evidence standard refers only to the final report. 11

There is another audit evidence standard that deserves mention. It applies to "performance audits" in the United States, which have most of the same objectives and characteristics as VFM audits in Canada. The General Accounting Office (GAO) evidence standard states that: 12

> Sufficient, competent, and relevant evidence is to be obtained to afford a reasonable basis for the auditors' judgments and conclusions regarding the organization, program, activity, or function under audit. A record of the auditors' work is to be retained in the form of working papers. Working papers may include tapes, films, and discs.[8]

Three differences are apparent between the wording of the Canadian and US standards, although the intended meaning appears to be very similar: 13

- the US standard uses the words *competent* and *relevant* instead of *appropriate* in describing the quality of evidence.
- the US standard describes evidence as being obtained to *afford a reasonable basis for the auditors' judgments and conclusions regarding the organization, program, activity, or function under audit*; the Canadian standard refers to evidence obtained *to afford a reasonable basis to support the content of the auditor's report.*
- the US standard includes specific references to documentation of the evidence in audit working papers.

SUFFICIENT AND APPROPRIATE

Determining what constitutes "sufficient" and "appropriate" evidence in a VFM audit is among the key decisions made by a VFM auditor; it has a major influence on the ultimate success or failure of the audit. Although these terms are not further defined in the *Value-for-Money Auditing Standards*, guidance on the meaning of the terms is contained in the CICA *Handbook*, which states that: 14

> As used in examination standard (iii), sufficiency is the measure of the quantity of audit evidence obtained and appropriateness is the measure of its quality.[9]
>
> The appropriateness, or quality, of audit evidence relates to its relevance and reliability. To be relevant, audit evidence must assist the auditor in achieving his audit objective. The reliability of audit evidence depends on its nature and source.[10]

As noted previously, the US evidence standard uses the terms *relevant* and *competent* rather than *appropriate*. Competent, in turn, is defined as *valid* and *reliable*. It is interesting to note that the terms relevant and reliable are also used to 15

---

8 GAO *Government Auditing Standards*, para. 57, p. 6-16.

9 CICA *Handbook*, Section 5300, Audit Evidence, para. .09.

10 *Ibid.*, para. .15.

describe evidence in a legal context — they are two of the tests that evidence must pass to be admissible in a court of law.

16 Although different terms are used in Canada and the United States to describe the measure of the quality of the audit evidence obtained, the meanings appear to be essentially the same. Similarities and differences will be explored more fully in a later chapter that assesses what constitutes sufficient and appropriate audit evidence.

FACTS, FINDINGS AND CONCLUSIONS

17 There are three terms that are used frequently in this study. They appear in the definitions of evidence quoted earlier and are essential to a discussion of VFM audit evidence.

18 *Facts* are directly linked to evidence — in some definitions, the terms are considered to be virtually synonymous. For example, evidence is described as "*facts* in support of a conclusion" and as "a collection of *facts*".

19 *Findings* and *conclusions* are also linked to both *facts* and to *evidence*. These terms are used, for example, in PSAAC's *Value-for-Money Auditing Standards*. In the paragraphs following the evidence standard, guidance is provided on ways of applying the standard (italics have been added for emphasis):

> In determining the sufficiency and appropriateness of evidence, the auditor is guided by the need to minimize the risk of reporting erroneous *findings* or inappropriate *conclusions*.[11]

20 The reporting standard for VFM audits includes the following references to the contents of the auditor's report:

> The auditor's report should ...identify the criteria and describe the findings which form the basis for the auditor's conclusions; and ...state the auditor's conclusions.[12]

21 To gain a clearer understanding of the intended meaning of *facts, findings* and *conclusions*, some dictionary definitions of these terms will be useful before proceeding further.

21 Definitions of *fact* include:

> something that actually exists; reality; truth.
>
> a truth known by actual experience or observation; something known to be true.[13]

22 Dictionary definitions of *finding(s)* include:

> something that is found or ascertained.
>
> a decision or verdict after judicial inquiry.[14]

---

[11] CICA Public Sector Auditing Statement 4, *Value-for-Money Auditing Standards*, para. .32.

[12] *Ibid.*, para. .37.

[13] Random House Dictionary.

[14] Random House Dictionary.

In addition, the GAO has defined *findings* as follows: 23

> The result of information development — a logical pulling together of information to arrive at conclusions (or a response to an audit objective on the basis of the sum of the information) about an organization, program, activity, function, condition, or other matter which was analyzed or evaluated. It need not be critical or be concerned only with deficiencies or weaknesses. A finding will be the basis for conclusions and recommendations for corrective action.[15]

Definitions of the term *conclusion(s)* include: 24

> the last main division of a discourse, usually containing a summing up of the points and a statement of opinion or decisions reached...
>
> a reasoned deduction or inference.
>
> a proposition concluded or inferred from the premises of an argument.[16]

For purposes of this study, the following definitions will be used: 25

- A *fact* is something that can be proven to be true;
- A *finding*, i.e., what has been found during the audit, is derived from one or more facts by applying professional judgment. A finding may also result from combining facts with other findings, or by combining two or more findings into another finding. An audit finding can be described as an intermediate conclusion;
- A *conclusion* is a statement in an auditor's report that summarizes the deductions arrived at by the auditor. Conclusions are derived from findings (which, in turn, are derived from facts) by the application of professional judgment. An *opinion*, for the purposes of this study, is regarded as being the same as a *conclusion*.

It will be apparent to the reader that these definitions do not provide a clear-cut distinction between findings and conclusions. Both rely on judgment and are ultimately based on facts established during the audit by the gathering of evidence. It is in this sense that a finding may be described as an intermediate conclusion. 26

Both terms, however, appear in the wording of the VFM auditing standards and are clearly intended to have different meanings. Accordingly, the Study Group has differentiated between them in this study and has found it useful to maintain that distinction in describing the nature and extent of evidence to be obtained during an audit. 27

---

15 GAO Government Auditing Standards, p. G-4.

16 Random House Dictionary.

28 The following chart illustrates potential linkages between facts and findings leading to a conclusion.

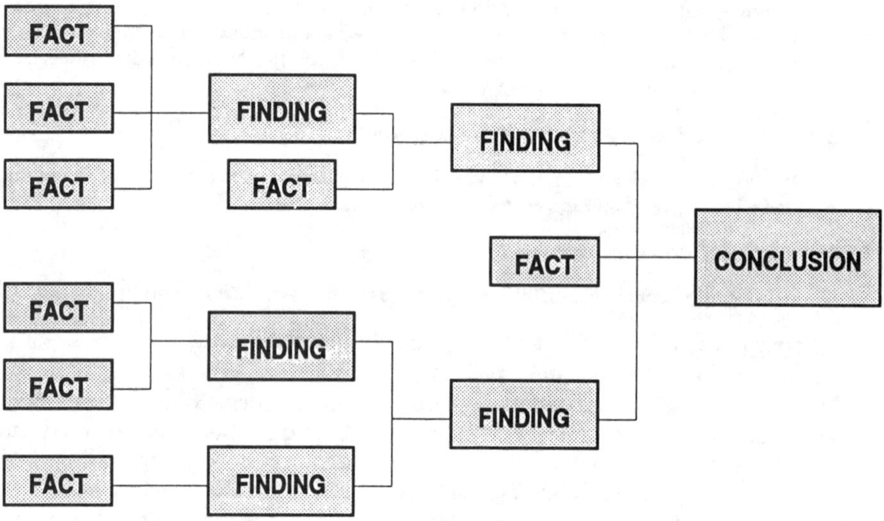

29 What is the purpose of making these distinctions? When discussing concepts of evidence, a framework is needed to answer the question, "evidence about what?" The distinctions and linkages between the terms facts, findings and conclusions that are illustrated above are not consistently used in current practice. Greater precision in the use of these terms by VFM audit practitioners in the future would be helpful to both auditors and readers of their reports.

30 This chapter has introduced some of the terms and evidence standards that provide a foundation for the discussion of evidence in later chapters. The next chapter will look at several alternative concepts of evidence and assess their applicability to VFM auditing.

Chapter 3

CONCEPTS OF EVIDENCE

INTRODUCTION

It is not difficult to identify the conceptual roots of auditing. Most of the theory and concepts that underlie current auditing practices were summarized in two landmark studies: Mautz and Sharaf's *The Philosophy of Auditing*,[1] published in 1961, and the American Accounting Association's *A Statement of Basic Auditing Concepts*,[2] published in 1973. 1

The *Philosophy of Auditing* attempted to place auditing theory on the foundation of classical concepts of logic, which support much of the theory developed in such diverse fields as science, medicine and law. These concepts deal with the way in which sound conclusions are reached, based on logical arguments. 2

Mautz and Sharaf's work led directly to *A Statement of Basic Auditing Concepts*. This later publication adopts many of the postulates and concepts developed in the earlier study, and uses them to formulate a number of basic auditing principles. This statement of principles, in turn, is reflected in the 1973 publication by the AICPA, *Statement on Auditing Standards*,[3] which contains the generally accepted auditing standards for business enterprises that have been adopted, virtually unchanged, in Canada. 3

Auditing concepts and practices in Canada have developed directly from the seminal works described above. Anderson's *The External Audit*,[4] the CICA Research Study, *Extent of Audit Testing*,[5] and more recent CICA studies all build on concepts first appearing in those earlier publications. 4

---

1 Mautz, R.K., Sharaf, H.A., *The Philosophy of Auditing*, American Accounting Association Monograph No. 6, 1961.

2 American Accounting Association, Studies in Accounting Research #6, *A Statement of Basic Auditing Concepts*, 1973.

3 AICPA, *Statement on Auditing Standards*, Codification of Auditing Standards and Procedures No. 1, 1973.

4 Anderson, R.J., *The External Audit*, Copp Clark Pitman, 1984 Second Edition.

5 CICA, *Extent of Audit Testing*, 1980.

BASIC AUDITING CONCEPTS

5 What are some of the concepts contained in these "bedrock" publications? It should be made clear from the outset that the concepts are mainly concerned with the auditor's opinion on "fair presentation" in a set of financial statements. Although the concepts are not restricted to financial statement attest audits, they are heavily influenced by auditing experience up to 1960, which was devoted almost exclusively to financial statement audits.

6 Mautz and Sharaf suggest that auditing applies the techniques and methods of proof:

> Proof is a part of the field of logic which has been described by some as the 'science of proof'. Logic is concerned with how we establish facts, conclusions, and inferences as valid or invalid. As such, logic is basic not only to auditing but also to law, which inevitably borrows its ideas and theories of proof from logic. In fact, any discipline which relies heavily on evidence is based on logic.[6]
>
> The practitioner of law or auditing must contemplate the essence of truth or proof or probability whenever he claims to be in search of the 'truth' in a given case, endeavors to obtain 'proof' of a given incident, or concludes that a certain inference has a given degree of 'probability'.[7]

They conclude, however, that legal evidence differs from audit evidence because there are important differences between the two professions.

7 In Chapter 5, Mautz and Sharaf discuss *The Nature of Evidence*,[8] the first of the fundamental concepts of auditing. Evidence is identified as:

- *Natural evidence* — evidence that physically exists; leads to "material truths" that leave no room for doubt.
- *Created evidence* — experimentation; analysis; leads to "mathematical truths", abstractions that can be as compelling as material truths (e.g., 2+2 = 4).
- *Rational argumentation* — ideas flowing logically from observed facts. This form of evidence is concerned only with the kind of knowledge obtained by inference or reasoning. The concept of "probability" is important to this form of evidence, a term used to indicate the relative certainty or uncertainty that a proposition is in accordance with reality.[9]

8 *A Statement of Basic Auditing Concepts* takes these ideas a step further. It discusses the "investigative process" (the term used to describe auditing) as follows:

> The auditor's role in the investigative process is to conduct an appropriate inquiry to determine the degree of credibility of certain propositions and to express an opinion on his findings. An opinion is an expression of the auditor's judgment or belief and, as such, represents an assertion of the proposition investigated. Assertion of the proposition is justified if it is declared and believed to be credible by the person asserting it. An assertion by a professional (a skilled investigator) implies that the

---

6 Mautz and Sharaf, p. 15.

7 *Ibid.*, p. 61.

8 *Ibid.*, pp. 68-110.

9 *Ibid.*, p. 72.

> assertion is warranted. A warranted assertion requires appropriate grounds for the belief; that is, the declared degree of belief should correspond to the degree of credibility.[10]

In discussing the criteria that justify a warranted assertion, the study refers to the *evident criterion*, that is, to the examination of evidence in support of propositions. Among the concepts discussed are the *competency* and *sufficiency* of audit evidence.[11] 9

VALUE-FOR-MONEY AUDITING CONCEPTS

Both of the studies referred to above, although their illustrations and much of their detailed guidance deal with financial statement attestation, try to place their underlying concepts in a broader context. For example, the *Statement of Basic Auditing Concepts* notes that: 10

> ...attestation is one possible output, and currently the most familiar output, of the audit process...the Committee would distinguish between the opinion formed in the audit of an accounting report (attestation) and an audit of managerial performance.[12]

Both of the above works recognize evidence as fundamental to auditing. They discuss, in some depth, the concepts that determine the quantity and quality of audit evidence to be gathered and evaluated in a financial statement audit. Much of the discussion of evidence centres on the concepts of probability, materiality, and the nature and extent of testing. Subsequent literature has developed much more comprehensive concepts of audit risk and materiality,[13] incorporating theories of mathematical probability and reliance on internal control. 11

These auditing concepts focus on the evidence required to enable an auditor to express an opinion on a set of financial statements. They provide financial statement auditors with a solid basis for determining the *sufficient appropriate* audit evidence needed to support their opinions. 12

VFM auditors also need *sufficient appropriate* audit evidence to support the content of their audit reports. The challenge, however, is to translate this statement into something more precise and definable that is useful to VFM practitioners, corresponding to the extensive methodology, standards and guidelines that have evolved in financial statement auditing to give concrete meaning to *sufficient* and *appropriate*.[14] 13

---

[10] *A Statement of Basic Auditing Concepts*, pp. 19-20.

[11] *Ibid.*, p. 29.

[12] *Ibid.*, p. 6.

[13] For example, the CICA Research Study by Donald A. Leslie, *Materiality: The Concept and its Application to Auditing*, 1985.

[14] Anderson's *The External Audit*, for example, contains charts and descriptions which provide a detailed, logically arranged and clearly described basis for determining what sufficient and appropriate mean in a financial statement audit.

14 Before proceeding to an assessment of alternative conceptual models that may be applicable to VFM auditing, there is another area that is relevant to the study of audit evidence, that of professional judgment.

PROFESSIONAL JUDGMENT

15 A key element in any assessment of audit evidence is the exercise of professional judgment. Professional judgment is applied throughout the audit process, and plays a particularly important role in the evaluation of evidence. In assessing the application of professional judgment in evaluating evidence, this study has relied to a large extent on research carried out by an earlier CICA Research Study, *Professional Judgment in Financial Reporting.*[15]

16 This earlier study provides a thorough analysis of the characteristics of professional judgment, including a comprehensive review of relevant literature. Much of this material can be applied directly to the professional judgment applied by a VFM auditor to audit evidence. Indeed, as the study points out, although little prior research had been done on professional judgment in financial reporting, research on professional judgment in auditing was fairly extensive.

17 The study defines professional judgment as "judgment exercised with due care, objectivity and integrity within the framework provided by accounting and other applicable standards, by experienced and knowledgeable people."[16] Research suggests that judgment is based on knowledge, experience, analysis and the particulars of the situation, and is affected by perceptions, risk, uncertainty, stress, consultation and learning.

18 The following excerpts from the study are considered to be particularly relevant to VFM audit evidence. One section of the study that requires mention because of its direct relevance is *A Process View of Professional Judgment.* It portrays the professional judgment process, and by inference the evaluation of VFM audit evidence, in the following way:

- The process takes place within an environment comprising legal, financial, risk, competitive and other factors. The environment offers both stability, support to habitual or routine judgment processes, and instability, changes that challenge or disrupt normal processes...
- Experience and knowledge make professionals continuously ready to respond as issues arise. The professional judgment process may therefore be considered to be continuous...this continuous process may be usefully segmented by identifying the event, perception, change or other "trigger" within the situation that sets the judgment process into operation. Analyzing the judgment process may be facilitated by identifying such a beginning and, at the other end, a resolution or ending, even though both are likely to be somewhat arbitrary...
- The situation also contains the data, the "facts", on which the judgment is, or should be, decided...

---

[15] Gibbins, Michael and Mason, Alister K., *Professional Judgment in Financial Reporting*, CICA 1988.

[16] *Ibid.*, p. 6.

- ...standards and rules play a crucial role. Their role exists with respect to both the situation (such as their presence, absence or clarity) and the people (for example, knowledge, experience, consensus)...
- ...judgment is a human process, with logical, psychological, social, legal and even political overtones...[17].

A simplified diagram of the influences on professional judgment is presented below.[18] 19

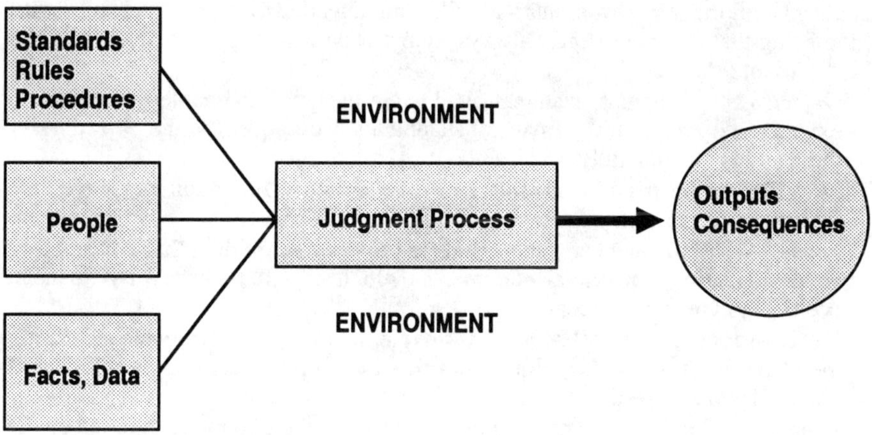

The judgment process is more complex and fluid than this flow diagram would suggest. Also, 20

> including people in the process requires consideration of perceptions, values, abilities, learning, expectations, and other human characteristics and differences.[19]

It is not practical to try to reproduce all of the other references in the study that could be applied to VFM audit evidence. Some of the most relevant excerpts, however, are contained in Appendix E. 21

AN ASSESSMENT OF ALTERNATIVE CONCEPTUAL MODELS

This study examines three concepts to assess their suitability as a foundation for VFM audit evidence: 22

- *Financial statement audit evidence* — Can the concepts of audit risk and materiality, reliance on internal control, and audit testing methods based on mathematical probability be adapted successfully to VFM auditing?

---

[17] *Ibid.*, p. 17.

[18] Adapted from *Professional Judgment in Financial Reporting*, Fig 3-1, p. 19.

[19] *Ibid.*, p. 23.

- *Legal evidence* — Earlier studies concluded that legal evidence concepts could not be applied successfully to financial statement audits. Does this also apply to VFM audits?
- *Logic and reasoning* — Can basic concepts of logic be successfully used to describe the nature of VFM audit evidence?

COMPARISON OF FINANCIAL STATEMENT AND VFM AUDITS

23 A reasonable starting point for an assessment of financial statement audit evidence concepts is to look at similarities and differences between VFM and financial statement auditing. The comments that follow are intended to reflect "typical" audits, recognizing that there are nearly always exceptions to overall summary statements about present practices.

- *Objectives* — Financial statement audits are designed to enable the auditor to express an opinion on the financial statements. Consequently, the objectives of these audits are generally consistent.

  VFM audits may be much more diverse and VFM audit objectives are typically quite different for each audit.
- *Scope* — The financial statement auditor provides an opinion that covers all of an organization's financial statements, which together portray its financial position and results of operations.

  The scope of each VFM audit is unique, and is generally developed during the planning phase of the audit, as information on the entity and its activities is gathered and assessed.
- *Criteria* — The auditor's opinion on a set of financial statements is based on the application of recognized criteria in the form of generally accepted accounting principles.

  VFM audit criteria are developed so as to correspond to the unique objectives and scope of each audit. The criteria are drawn from authoritative sources and reflect good management practice, but they are not considered to be "generally accepted" in the sense of formal acceptance by all or most practitioners.
- *Significance/materiality and risk* — The related concepts of materiality and risk have a profound effect on the conduct of financial statement audits. These audits are designed to reduce audit risk, expressed in quantitative terms, to an acceptably low percentage. For example, the CICA guideline on materiality and audit risk states that "...it is suggested that most auditors expressing audit risk in quantitative terms would strive to limit such risk to no more than 5%".[20]

  It is not possible to make a similar definitive statement about VFM audits (even though materiality and risk play an important part) since audit risk can rarely be expressed in solely quantitative terms.
- *Form of conclusion/opinion* — Most financial statement auditors' reports include a standard short-form audit opinion. This reflects the consistent nature of the audit objectives and the relatively fixed nature of the audit scope.

---

[20] CICA *Handbook*, Auditing Guideline, *Applying materiality and audit risk concepts in conducting an audit*, March 1990, p. 5, para. .16.

Most VFM auditors, on the other hand, do not use a standard form of opinion. Their reports are much longer, have no standard format and contain a series of conclusions (often related to individual audit projects) rather than a single conclusion. Some conclusions in VFM audit reports are labelled as such, or are stated in explicit terms that make it clear they are conclusions. Other reports do not label their conclusions and the conclusions may in fact be implied rather than specifically stated.

- *Evidence* — Evidence standards in financial statement and VFM audits contain virtually identical wording. In practice, however, the words "sufficient and appropriate" have been applied quite differently.

  Evidence is obtained by methods such as inspection, observation, enquiry, confirmation and analysis, used in both financial statement and VFM audits. The emphasis given to these techniques, however, as, for example, in the use of third party confirmations or the use of interviews, can be significantly different.
- *Quantitative and qualitative approaches to gathering and evaluating audit evidence* — Financial statement audits employ both quantitative and qualitative approaches. For example, Section 5130 of the CICA *Handbook* recognizes that, "the determination of materiality involves qualitative as well as quantitative considerations."[21] The emphasis in financial statement audits, however, is predominantly quantitative. This is understandable, since the objective of the audit is to provide an opinion on the financial statements, whose unit of measurement is dollars (or some other currency). Errors are also usually stated as quantities, either in dollars or percentages. Gathering evidence to support the audit opinion directs the auditor towards quantitative techniques to establish the accuracy of the amounts in the financial statements.[22]

  VFM audits also use both quantitative and qualitative approaches.[23] The emphasis in VFM audits is on the audit of management performance, not of amounts. Although the verification of amounts expressed in dollars or some other unit of measurement is part of most VFM audits, it is generally not the primary focus. The emphasis in a VFM audit, therefore, is predominantly qualitative.

In summary, financial statement audits are based on risk assessment, evaluating internal controls, audit tests and confidence levels expressed as percentages. These audits emphasize quantitative measures and typically result in a short-form report using standard wording for the auditor's opinion, regardless of the organization being audited. 24

Value-for-money audits, on the other hand, emphasize qualitative measures, resulting in a long-form report that is tailored to the particular circumstances of each audit. Standards in both cases refer to evidence obtained "to afford a reasonable basis to support the content of the auditor's report", but the "content of the report" is dissimilar in almost all respects. 25

---

[21] CICA *Handbook, Materiality and audit risk in conducting an audit*, Section 5130, para. .07.

[22] "Fair presentation" in the financial statements includes explanatory information as well as amounts, information that is likely to be largely qualitative in nature. Nevertheless, the primary emphasis in the audit is usually quantitative.

[23] CICA Public Sector Auditing Statement 4, *Value-for-Money Auditing Standards*, para. .22.

26 Many techniques developed for financial statement audits will be appropriate in particular circumstances for VFM audits. Where this is the case, guidance provided in the CICA *Handbook*, Guidelines and Research Studies will be applicable. There are also obvious similarities in the types of evidence and methods of gathering evidence, and portions of Section 5300 of the Handbook on Audit Evidence apply equally to VFM and financial statement audits.

27 What can one conclude from this comparison? The Study Group has suggested that most of the basic elements of a financial statement audit differ in some respect from those of a VFM audit. The similarity in the wording of the two audit evidence standards, however, does not reflect these basic differences.

28 Financial statement audits are built around the concept of mathematical probability. This concept does not work nearly as well for VFM auditing. The number of variables that exist in VFM audits appear to make it impossible on any practical basis to assess audit risk in quantitative terms. Fundamental differences in the content of the auditor's report also suggest that different audit concepts are needed for the evidence gathered in support of the VFM auditor's conclusions.

29 The emphasis on quantitative measures in financial statement auditing is undergoing re-examination in some quarters, perhaps because of increased emphasis on "fair presentation", which has important qualitative as well as quantitative implications.

30 Academic literature on audit evidence was fairly common at the time that sections of the Handbook related to audit evidence were under discussion and development.[24] This literature speculated on various quantitative approaches to determining the meaning of "sufficient and appropriate evidence" in a financial statement audit.

31 Recent literature has suggested that the mathematical model previously advocated, which had the apparent advantage of scientific logic and precision, may be suspect since it does not adequately deal with qualitative measures in financial statements.[25]

---

[24] See for example: A General Theory of Evidence as the Conceptual Foundation in Auditing Theory, by Yoshihide Toba, *The Accounting Review*, January, 1975, pp. 7-24; comments and extensions on the theory by John N. Kissinger and Thomas E. Gibbs, *The Accounting Review*, April and July,1977; An Investigation of the Descriptiveness of the General Theory of Evidence and Auditing, Ray G. Stephens, *Auditing: A Journal of Practice & Theory*, pp. 55-74, Fall 1983; and *Research in Audit Decision Making: Rationale, Evidence, and Implications*, Robert H. Ashton, The Canadian Certified General Accountants' Research Foundation, 1983.

[25] Smieliauskas,Wally and Smith, Lloyd, "A theory of evidence based on audit assertions", *Contemporary Accounting Research*, Vol. 6, No. 2, pp. 407-426, Spring 1990, concluded that:

> We have provided an improved framework for a theory of evidence in auditing. The major contribution here is the crucial role that explanations play in this theory and the discussion of the various qualitative dimensions of explanations: social acceptability, entrenchment, pragmatic notion, situational context, and the role of quantitative models. This explanatory factor provides an understanding as to why purely quantitative models of auditing may not be sufficient for developing a theory of audit evidence. ...Explanations thus provide an important heretofore ignored factor associated with audit quality. Our theoretical framework suggests that improved audit quality may be achieved by providing guidance on what constitutes appropriate explanations in common or particularly risky audit circumstances.

LEGAL EVIDENCE

Any mention of evidence brings to many people's minds visions of Perry Mason and courtroom dramas played out in detective novels, on the movie screen and on television. Many have participated directly in the judicial system through appearances as jurors, witnesses, experts or observers. 32

Through these and other sources of information, people have a general understanding of the importance of legal evidence in criminal and civil court cases, as well as a general familiarity with legal terms associated with evidence — "admissible" or "inadmissible" evidence, "circumstantial" evidence, and so on. 33

The legal system provides the most intense forum for the practice and analysis of reasoning. Legal reasoning focuses primarily on what the "facts" are — that is, what will be accepted as "facts" for the purposes of legal decision making. 34

The legal system is an adversary process. Each party is free to present the case and to define the issues in dispute. After the court has received all the evidence submitted by the parties, each party has the right to make legal arguments based on the evidence. The law of evidence guides and controls the parties in such matters. 35

In a civil court case, evidence must be presented to substantiate "issues of fact". The evidence can be in the form of testimony by witnesses or it can be physical evidence such as documents or records. The conclusions drawn by the judge or jury in the case (the verdict) will be based on their assessment of the issues of fact that have been established. 36

Probability plays an important role in establishing "facts". There is a higher standard of proof required in a criminal case ("beyond reasonable doubt") than in a civil case ("the balance of probabilities"). It is important to note that the legal system has resisted efforts to introduce standards to measure probability. Appellate court decisions have reaffirmed that it is individual judgment that is to be applied in determining the meaning to be given to "beyond reasonable doubt" or "the balance of probabilities" in a particular case, not reference to a standard of measurement that can be applied. 37

The concept of legal evidence has many parallels in VFM audit evidence: 38

- Oral evidence is very important.[26] The most frequent source of grounds in a legal case is the testimony of witnesses — those with first hand knowledge of matters in dispute. This testimony is subject to cross-examination to test its credibility and consistency. It is tested again by the rules of evidence — is it relevant and material? The testimony of experts is admissible in court, and is also subject to cross-examination and challenge.

  In VFM auditing, there is extensive use of interviews with knowledgeable individuals. These individuals are subject to questioning by the auditor and cross-checking to other interviews and corroborating data. Information provided

---

[26] It is interesting to note that oral evidence is described as testimonial evidence in the GAO Government Auditing Standards, pp. 6-16.

is tested for credibility and consistency. Expert opinions are also sought in many VFM audits, and these opinions are subject to critical review and challenge.

- The terminology is similar. The vocabulary of audit evidence parallels that of the legal system — *evidence, facts* and *findings* are part of the judicial as well as the audit process. Other terms are also common to both. For example, *relevancy* is an important attribute of both legal and audit evidence.
- For both legal and VFM audits, evidence is an essential element in "building a case" on the basis of established facts. A process of challenge and discovery takes place in both settings and the reasoning processes involved are complex and unpredictable.
- Both disciplines place great importance on screening evidence so that conclusions are reached based on relevant and reliable evidence. In a court case, evidence that is not relevant to the facts in issue, or unreliable evidence such as hearsay evidence, will not be admissible as a basis for reaching a verdict. Similarly, in a VFM audit, it is of prime importance for the auditor to gather evidence that is relevant to the audit objectives, and that does not include faulty data or unsubstantiated allegations.
- Finally, both the legal system and VFM auditing use probability concepts to determine conclusions based on facts. Both rely on "persuasive" rather than "conclusive" evidence to establish the propositions that are put forward to be analyzed and assessed.

39 Although there are similarities, a word of caution is in order. There are also significant differences between the concepts of legal and VFM audit evidence. The legal process is an adversary system that depends on arguments being presented both for and against the matters to be decided. Neither side is expected to be objective in preparing its case. The process is subject to the rules of evidence which, if not followed, can result in a decision being appealed and in some cases overturned. There are also rules on testimony under oath and rights of cross-examination that clearly have no parallel in VFM audits.

40 These are such fundamentally different approaches to "building a case" that it is evident that it would be unwise for VFM auditors to adopt the legal model, even though some of the methods of obtaining and evaluating evidence are similar and can be usefully applied.

41 Additional observations on the nature of legal evidence are contained in Appendix E.

LOGIC AND REASONING

42 The Study Group has looked at financial statement evidence and legal evidence as they relate to VFM auditing. Financial statement audits have many important similarities, but there are also important differences. Concepts of legal evidence have parallels to VFM evidence, but this study has concluded that the legal model is not appropriate.

43 Of course, each of these preceding discussions has a common base. Each deals with the process for reaching rational conclusions based on evidence. It is now time to turn to the underlying concept that encompasses all forms of decision-making —

logic and reasoning. As described earlier in this chapter, logic concepts have provided the basis for the development of basic auditing concepts.

This study does not intend to try to summarize all that has been written about logic and reasoning. The Study Group is not presumptuous enough to attempt a neat précis in a field where there is much philosophical debate and controversy. Nevertheless, a few general observations are in order. 44

The study of logic began at the time of Aristotle, who wrote: 45

> As a start, we must say what this inquiry is about and to what subject it belongs; namely, that it is concerned with *apodeixes* [i.e. the way in which conclusions are to be established] and belongs to the science *(episteme)* of their establishment.[27]

Various attempts have been made to develop a theory of logic based on scientific principles. Some models have been developed based on mathematical probability, others using behavioral science as a model. None have gained universal acceptance. This approach has also led to the use of mathematical probability measures in providing support for conclusions — a logical progression in the use of the concept. This concept has been applied, as this study has already noted, to evidence supporting financial statement audit opinions. 46

At the beginning of this chapter, in commenting on basic auditing concepts, the study noted that auditing applies the techniques and methods of proof; proof is a part of the field of logic. Logic theory also describes the means by which persuasive arguments are constructed and valid conclusions are reached. Other important logic concepts are those of probability and logical fallacies. In summary, logic theory provides the basic framework for the development of a logic model for VFM audit evidence. 47

This study has stressed the fact that the mathematical orientation of financial statement auditing concepts has made them inappropriate as models for VFM auditing. Some students of logic have also questioned attempts to use "scientific" logic in complex areas of judgment where it may not be appropriate. Quotations from two of these scholars, Stephen Toulmin and Jonathan Cohen, both authors of texts on logical arguments, are included in Appendix E. 48

Both Cohen and Toulmin view legal arguments and legal evidence as having implications for everyday reasoning and logic. Toulmin has gone a step further and, using legal terminology, has constructed a logic model that he believes can be applied to any form of reasoning, including legal reasoning, argumentation in science, arguing about the arts and ethical reasoning. The analytical diagram used as a framework by Toulmin to explain his reasoning concept is outlined on the next page.[28] 49

---

[27] Quoted in Toulmin, Stephen, *The Uses of Argument*, Cambridge University Press, 1958, p. 2.

[28] Toulmin S., Rieke R., and Janik A., *An Introduction to Reasoning*, Second Edition, Macmillan Publishing, 1984, p. 98.

50 In narrative form, the model shows that "given grounds G, one may appeal to warrant W (which rests on backing B) to justify the claim that C — or, at any rate, the presumption (Q) that C — in the absence of some specific rebuttal or disqualification R."[29]

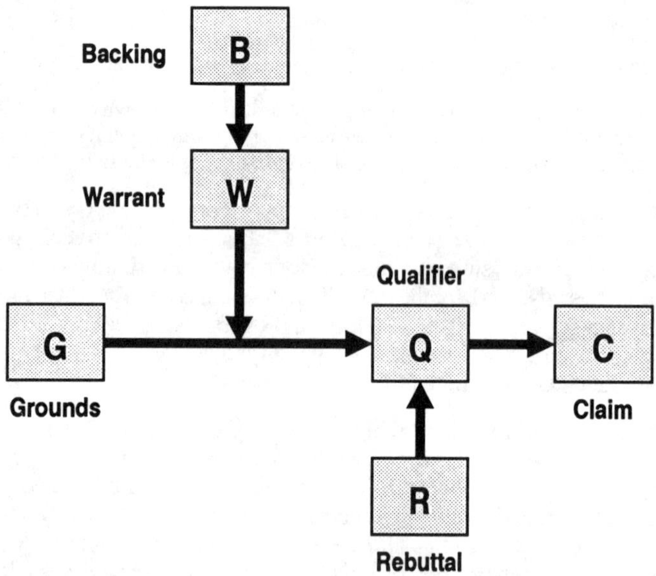

51 The terms used in the model are described as follows:

- *Claim* — Assertions put forward for general acceptance (the opinion or conclusion);
- *Grounds* — The generally accepted and relevant "facts" on which the claim is based (the evidence);
- *Warrants* — The general laws, rules or principles that make these facts relevant to the claim (the rationale/criteria supporting the claim);
- *Backing* — The support that makes explicit the body of experience relied on to establish the trustworthiness of the warrants presented (the authorities supporting the rationale/criteria);
- *Qualifiers* — Phrases that show what kind of, and degree of, reliance is to be placed on the conclusions, given the arguments available to support them. These consist of adverbs and adverbial phrases such as: necessarily, certainly, presumably, in all probability, very likely, very possibly, apparently, and so on.
- *Rebuttals* — Extraordinary or exceptional circumstances that might undermine the force of the supporting arguments.

---

[29] *Ibid.*, p. 98.

A couple of examples taken from *An Introduction to Reasoning* may help to illustrate the use of the model: 52

Example One
A meteorological illustration

The weather will be clearing and cooler by tomorrow morning.[30]

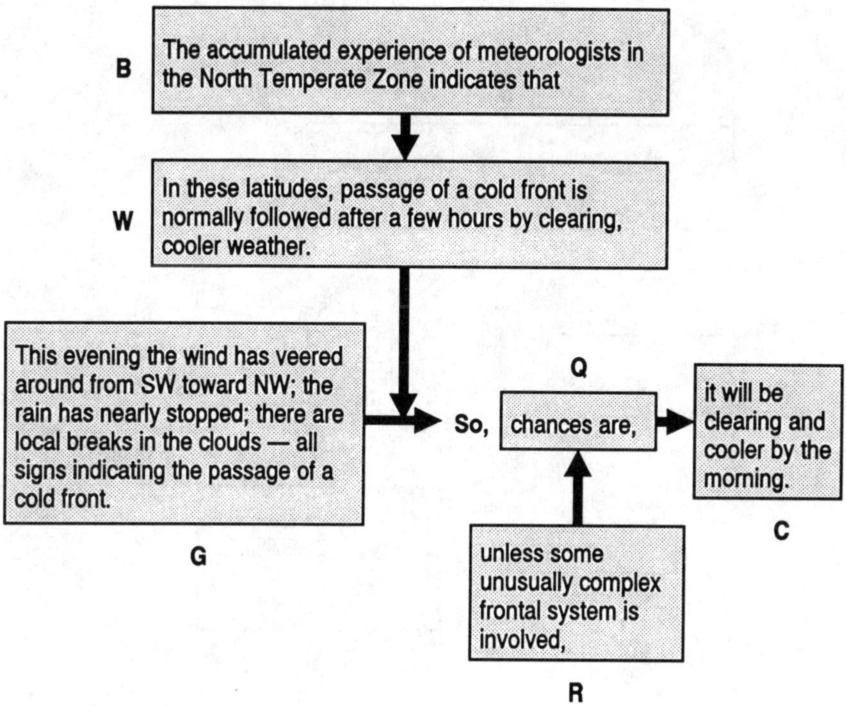

[30] *Ibid.*, p. 124.

Example Two
A medical argument

A patient turns up at the doctor's office with a sore throat, a headache, and a running nose that will not clear up. The physician recognizes the symptoms as frequently associated with a bacterial infection of the upper respiratory tract.[31]

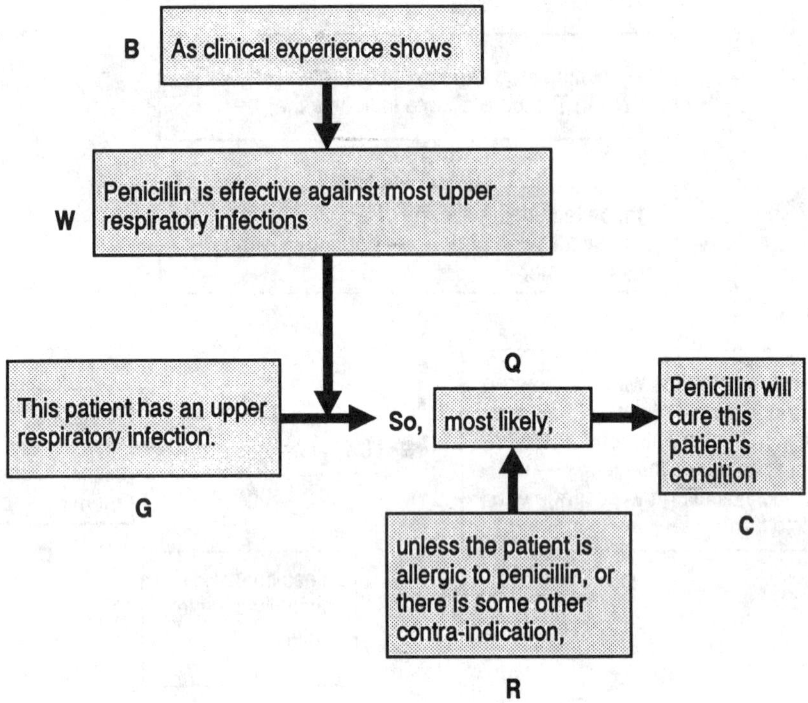

[31] *Ibid.*, p. 83.

A further example of the use of the logic model that may be familiar to those readers with an audit background is the following: 53

Example Three
A financial statement audit logic model

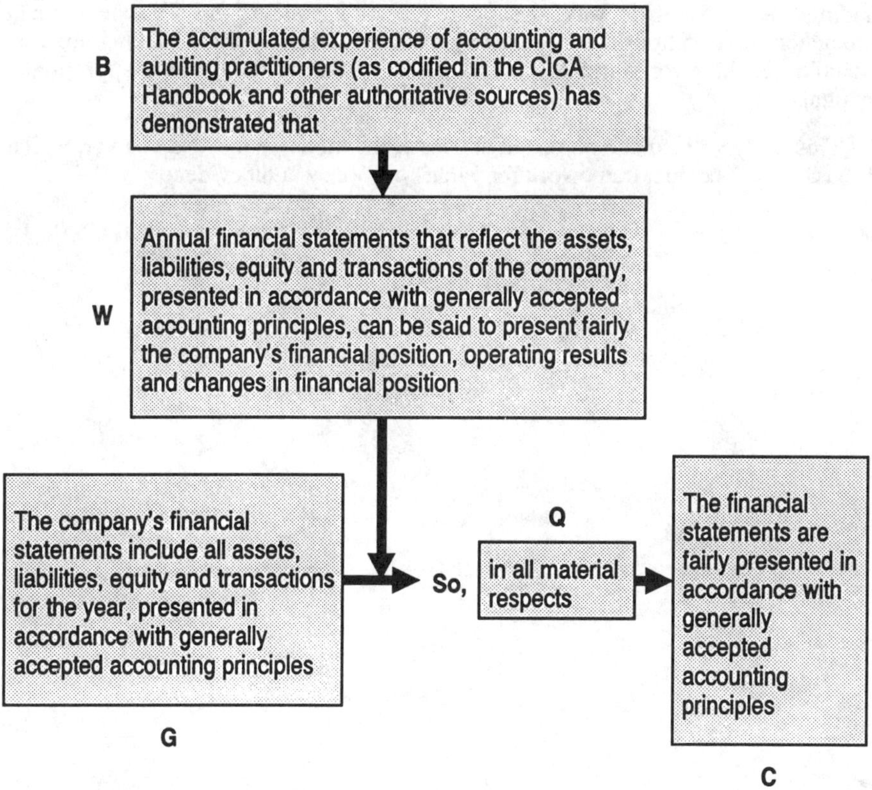

This is all very interesting — but what does it have to do with VFM auditing? Can this concept be applied to VFM audit evidence? This study has concluded that the answer is yes — this concept is well-suited for modelling the VFM audit process. 54

Consider some of the basic features of VFM audits: 55

- VFM audits emphasize qualitative rather than quantitative considerations;
- building support for a VFM audit conclusion is one form of constructing a logical argument;
- VFM audits involve an assessment of probabilities as do other audits, but in most instances these audits do not lend themselves to extensive use of mathematical probability concepts. This is particularly true in the case of evidence supporting conclusions.

56 These factors have led the Study Group to conclude that the use of a logic model that links "grounds" and "claims" is appropriate. They believe that such a model can help to explain the attributes of VFM audit evidence and assist in assessing what constitutes sufficient appropriate audit evidence in a VFM audit.

57 There is another potential benefit from using the model. By breaking an argument, or proposition, into its components, the auditor can marshall the facts and findings in a systematic way to support the audit conclusions. The auditor can strengthen the weight of the evidence by using a rational decision-making process, including backing for warrants, careful use of qualifiers, and, where appropriate, rebuttals.

58 This study will expand on potential uses of the model in the next chapter, which discusses a conceptual framework for value-for-money audit evidence.

Chapter 4

A CONCEPTUAL FRAMEWORK FOR VALUE-FOR-MONEY AUDIT EVIDENCE

VFM AUDIT LOGIC MODEL

The wording of the VFM audit evidence standard has been referred to frequently in this study, in particular the term "sufficient appropriate audit evidence". A key issue for the study is the need for a clear understanding as to what sufficient appropriate evidence means in a VFM audit context. To obtain this understanding, the nature of the support required for VFM audit findings and conclusions must be assessed. 1

This study has concluded that the interpretation given to sufficient and appropriate in a financial statement audit cannot be applied successfully to most VFM audits. Instead, the process of building support for a conclusion using concepts of logic has been advocated. 2

To illustrate these concepts, a simple VFM audit logic model is shown below, using terms appropriate for auditing, rather than the terms used in the previous chapter. The model concentrates on the link between facts and findings, but the model is equally applicable to the reasoning process followed in reaching conclusions based on audit findings. Two additional boxes have been added to the model, procedures and conclusions, to help place it in a VFM audit context. 3

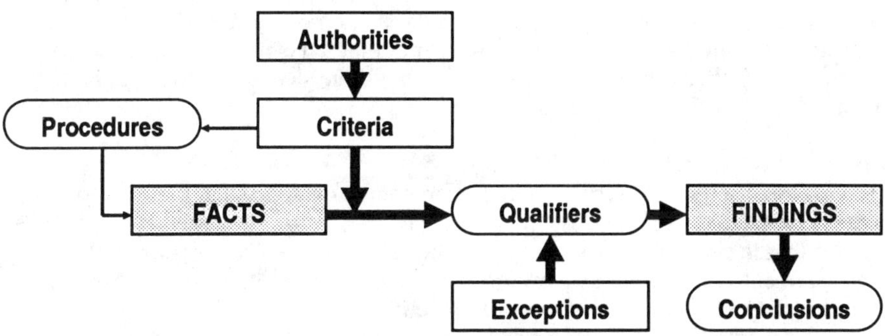

4 Before considering how this logic model can be applied to VFM auditing, a few preliminary comments are necessary.

5 The reasoning process that the auditor goes through in arriving at a finding or conclusion and the support provided in the auditor's report depend on persuasive evidence that the finding or conclusion is "logical". The logic model is a means of breaking down this reasoning process into its components. By so doing, a better understanding of what constitutes "persuasive" support can be gained.

6 In practice, the reasoning process involved in mulling over findings, developing and discarding potential causes and possible effects and formulating conclusions is ongoing and largely intuitive, rather than following rigid rules of logic. The purpose of the model, therefore, is not to suggest that an auditor's thought process should somehow be modified to follow a set pattern, but instead to demonstrate the elements in building a persuasive audit conclusion.

7 Failure to carefully describe the facts, findings and conclusions in an auditor's report (for example, by failing to state an exception or by using an inappropriate qualifier) may result in the report being misinterpreted. Alternatively, a review of the logic supporting the conclusion may reveal that the logic is flawed and that the support for the conclusion should be re-examined.

8 The components of the VFM audit logic model are discussed in the paragraphs that follow.

Procedures

9 The logic model includes the audit *procedures*, the means by which the audit evidence is gathered.

Facts

10 The evidence establishes the *facts* that appear in the audit report (the term "facts" includes all the descriptions, background information, data and other observations which together provide the support for the audit findings).

Criteria

11 Professional judgment is applied to the facts, which are compared with the *criteria* established for the audit. This evaluation of evidence cannot be viewed as a sequential process with defined steps. The exact process by which right or wrong conclusions are reached is not capable of precise definition. In moving from facts to findings, therefore, the auditor will be conscious of both the facts obtained, and the criteria against which they are being compared. Both will influence the findings that result from this logical thought process.

Authorities

12 The criteria used must be supported by convincing evidence that they are based on accepted practice, established policy or procedures, or are supported by some other source that is generally acknowledged to be authoritative. This support will usually be documented in the audit working papers, rather than described as part of the auditor's report. Without this support, the criteria that are applied during the audit may lack credibility, affecting the persuasiveness of the findings and conclusions.

Exceptions

13 The persuasiveness of a set of findings will also be enhanced by recognizing situations where the conclusion reached may not apply. To state a set of findings in terms that suggest that there are no exceptions will detract from the credibility of the findings if they are later challenged. It is important to state significant exceptions, so that the findings do not appear to be undermined by cases that are isolated instances. By stating exceptions as part of the description of the findings, the reader is provided with better information on which to base an assessment of the matters reported.

Qualifiers

14 In describing findings, care should be taken to use the appropriate adverbs or adverbial phrases. For example, an occurrence should not be described as "usually" happening (most of the time), when in fact it "frequently" happens (many times, but not necessarily most of the time). Similarly, the phrase "in all probability" suggests virtual certainty that a set of findings is correct; the term "probably" implies less certainty.

15 The purpose of these qualifying words or phrases in the description of the findings is to express in as clear a way as possible the "degree of certainty" that the auditor attaches to the findings. The importance of these words and phrases should not be underestimated. The acceptability of a set of findings often depends on the words used to describe it, not just on the evidence gathered to support it.

Findings

16 In simple terms, this is a statement of what was found during the audit. In some reports, it may be described as an observation or sometimes an assertion (this would be an appropriate term for a statement originally made by the auditee and subsequently confirmed by the auditor). The conversion of facts to findings is both simultaneous and iterative. Information gathered during interviews, by reviewing reports, etc., will often cover a variety of subjects. The subject matter may be covered by more than one criterion and may eventually result in more than one finding. In addition, a new finding may result in a rethinking of earlier findings.

Conclusions

17 This study has already referred to various combinations of facts and findings eventually leading to an audit conclusion. The auditor's report will generally contain several conclusions for each audit. These conclusions should be related to the objectives and scope of the audit and should follow logically from the description of the criteria and findings.

ILLUSTRATIONS OF THE LOGIC MODEL

18 The following charts illustrate the use of the logic model as an analytical tool in evaluating audit evidence. (The facts and criteria in the examples have been simplified, since the objective is to illustrate the model, not suitable criteria).

19 The models are intended to serve two purposes:

- to set out the components of an "argument" in an audit report; i.e., the way in which a set of findings is developed based on the facts that have been gathered;

- to show the relationship between the components in arriving at a "persuasive" set of findings; i.e., the comparison of facts with criteria to provide logical and persuasive support for the findings.

20 As a result of the audit of a training program for inspectors, the auditor found that the criteria, with one exception, had been met. The way in which this judgment was arrived at can be portrayed as follows:

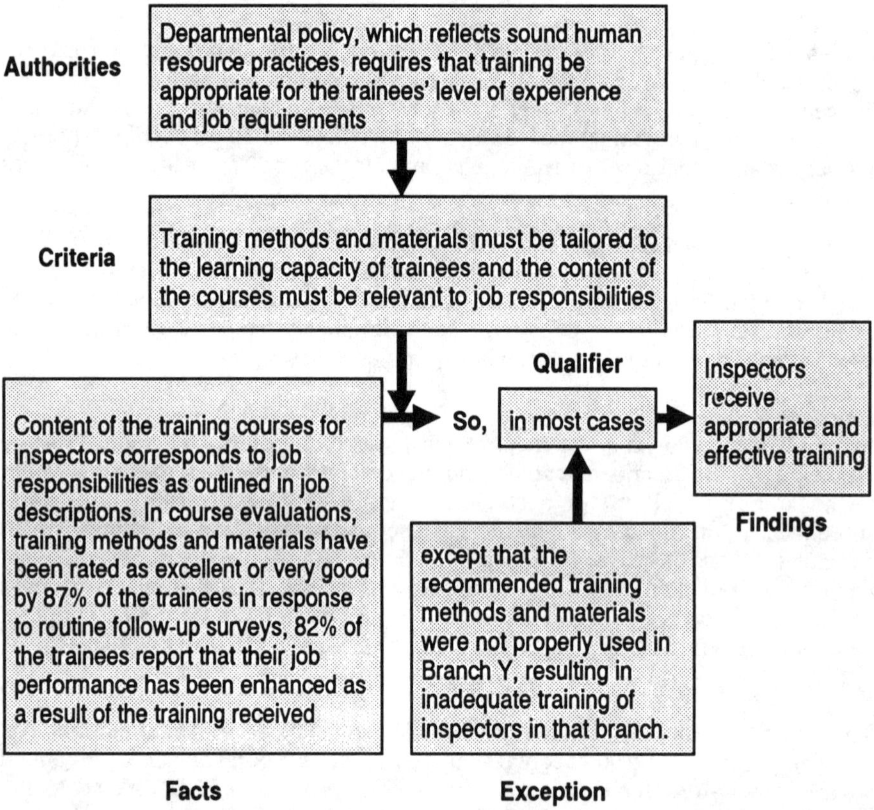

Another example of the use of the model is as follows: 21

An audit has been conducted on the construction of a new facility.

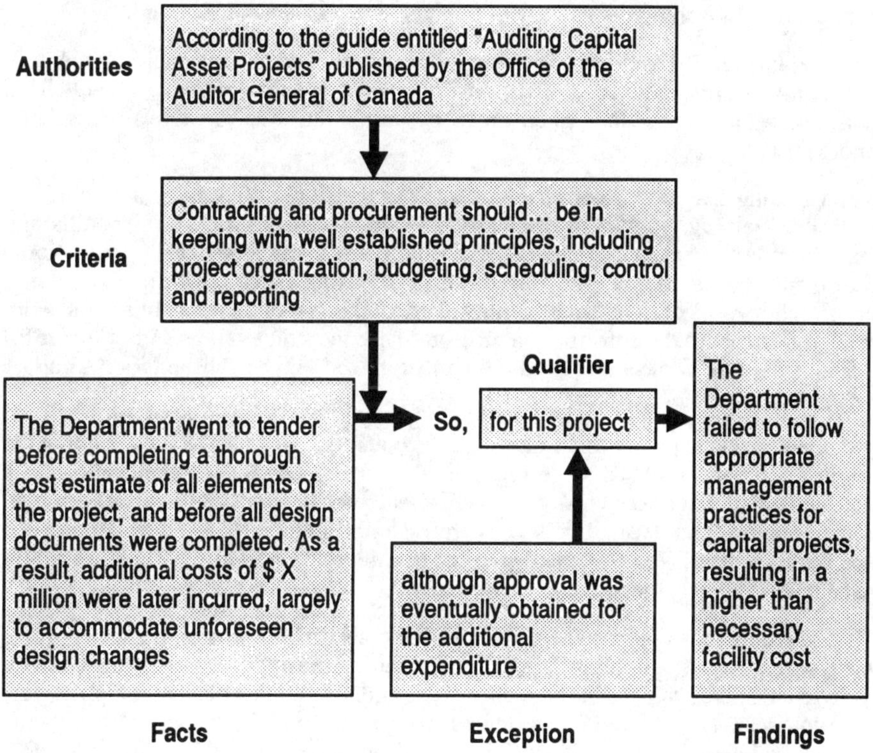

NATURE OF EVIDENCE

One further explanation is needed before proceeding. Dictionary definitions of 22
evidence are necessarily fairly broad, such as "that which tends to prove or disprove something", "ground for belief" or "facts in support of a conclusion". In VFM auditing, the term evidence is often used to describe various types of data gathered during the audit, as well as arguments presented in support of a conclusion. For purposes of this study, however, our discussion will focus on the evidence needed to support the content of the auditor's report.

Support for Facts, Findings and Conclusions

The emphasis in this study is on the development of findings and conclusions, derived 23
from facts, which typically represents the most difficult part of the audit. Many of the characteristics that distinguish facts, findings and conclusions have already been discussed. The feature of most importance to this study, however, is the differing

degrees of credibility associated with each, i.e., the differing probability that a fact, finding or conclusion is correct. This difference reflects the strength of the evidence supporting the facts, findings and conclusions.

24 Facts must be supported by strong evidence. Although absolute proof rarely exists, facts must be supported by evidence that will withstand challenge and is capable of establishing the validity of the fact "beyond reasonable doubt".

25 Findings are derived from facts by the application of professional judgment. In addition to findings based directly on established facts, findings can result from combining facts with other findings, or by combining two or more findings into another finding.

26 A finding may be virtually certain, such as the finding that there is a failure to institute a training program as originally planned. In other cases, a finding, although supported by persuasive evidence, may involve a greater degree of professional judgment. For example, the auditor may develop criteria for the audit of a construction project. The auditor may then obtain proof that establishes several related facts about the construction project. These facts, in total, provide support for a finding that the project met (or did not meet) the criteria established for the audit.

27 Conclusions are derived from findings by the application of professional judgment. Conclusions in this context are the opinions expressed by the auditor in the auditor's report, such as a description of a deficiency with an accompanying recommendation, or a conclusion as to whether or not an audit criterion has been met. Since conclusions are usually based on professional judgment to a greater degree than are findings, it follows that the degree of certainty attached to the conclusion will usually be somewhat less.

28 For example, using the illustration of the construction project, there may have been several construction projects examined during the audit. Each may result in an individual finding which, in total, allows the auditor to conclude that a higher level criterion related to capital expenditures has (or has not) been met. Although the auditor believes that there is sufficient evidence to support this conclusion, that support will not usually have the same degree of certainty as the evidence which supports findings on individual projects.

Support for Objectives, Scope, Criteria, Recommendations and Management's Responses Contained in the Auditor's Report

29 There are other items in the auditor's report besides facts, findings and conclusions. These include the audit objectives, scope and criteria and, where they are included in the report, recommendations and management's responses. The evidence required to support these items is of a different nature to that needed to support facts, findings and conclusions. The support consists primarily of the analysis carried out at the time the decisions on these items were made, supplemented by data that may have entered into the decisions.

30 The objectives, scope and criteria are determined during the planning phase of the audit. Support for these items will be obtained and documented at that time. Support for recommendations included in the auditor's report, to the extent that it is required,

will be obtained and documented during the preparation of the report. The nature and extent of evidence required for each of these items will be discussed further in the next chapter.

If management's responses have been included in the auditor's report, they are presented as the views of management rather than representing the opinions of the auditor. As such, they are not required to be supported by audit evidence. If the comments include statements that the auditor believes to be factually incorrect, however, it is the view of the Study Group that the auditor has an obligation to obtain evidence either to confirm or refute this belief. If confirmed, the auditor should discuss the matter with management and take any further action considered necessary. 31

Much of the discussion of evidence to this point has been fairly general and has dealt with evidence concepts rather than techniques for obtaining evidence in a VFM audit. In succeeding chapters, the study will take a closer look at the nature of evidence, first examining in detail the meaning of sufficient and appropriate VFM audit evidence, then focusing on specific types and sources of evidence and important factors to consider when evaluating VFM audit evidence. 32

Chapter 5

SUFFICIENT APPROPRIATE AUDIT EVIDENCE

INTRODUCTION

So far, evidence has been described in general terms. There is a good reason for this. The auditor must have a clear understanding of the concepts that determine what constitutes sufficient and appropriate value-for-money audit evidence before attempting to consider the questions: 1

- what kind of evidence is needed, and
- what techniques should be used to obtain that evidence?

STAGES OF THE AUDIT

A review of the VFM audit process is a useful first step in assessing sufficient and appropriate audit evidence. It is not an objective of this study, however, to attempt to define a "standard" process or to include all of the steps that one might expect to find as part of the process. 2

The process of gathering evidence is ongoing throughout the audit. Some evidence will be used to support the findings and conclusions, other evidence will be assessed as irrelevant or unreliable and set aside. The sequence in which evidence is gathered varies between audits and often between auditors. 3

The following chart illustrates the major steps in the VFM audit process.[1] 4

---

[1] This chart is an abbreviated version of Exhibit 1301.1, "Overview of Audit Process", contained in the Comprehensive Audit Manual of the Office of the Auditor General of Canada issued in 1990.

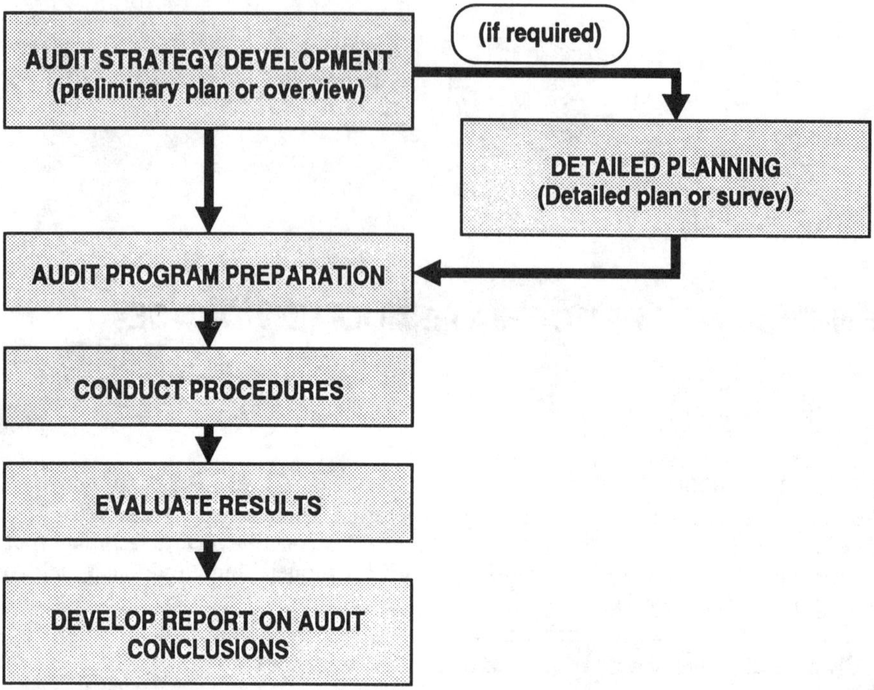

5 Much of the audit evidence is obtained during the examination phase of the audit, following the preparation of audit programs. Some evidence, however, may be obtained during the planning phase, while other evidence may be obtained as the final report is being written. For example, during the initial planning meeting, documents may be available which represent evidence supporting a statement that eventually appears in the final report. At the other extreme, in the process of clearing the final report, it may be determined that stronger support is required for a particular fact, finding or conclusion, and additional evidence will be obtained.

6 After the evidence has been obtained, it must be evaluated. Part of this evaluation takes place throughout the audit, as evidence is assessed for relevance and reliability. It is generally on completion of the examination, however, that an overall assessment takes place of the sufficiency and appropriateness of audit evidence.

7 In some cases, this evidence will not be convincing enough to support the facts, findings or conclusions in the report. In other situations, evidence of a contradictory nature may be obtained, casting doubt on the validity of a fact, finding or conclusion. In either case, additional evidence will be required and another evaluation must take place (or the fact, finding or conclusion will have to be dropped).

8 Important decisions in a VFM audit usually revolve around an evaluation of evidence, since the persuasiveness of the findings and conclusions in the auditor's

report often depend upon choices made by the auditor at the end of the examination phase of the audit.

VALUE-FOR-MONEY AUDIT EVIDENCE LOGIC MODEL

This study has approached the topic of VFM audit evidence from several directions — by reviewing the nature of the evidence required to support the "content of the auditor's report", by assessing the differing degrees of support required, and by developing a series of models to better understand VFM audit evidence concepts. 9

These ideas have been brought together in a single model, presented as a representation of a "typical" VFM audit. This model includes the components of the auditor's report that are recommended by PSAAC's *Value-for-Money Auditing Standards*.[2] The model highlights the critical decision points in a VFM audit. These decision points are numbered and are described more fully in the following section. The evidence required at each of these stages of the audit is also described. 10

The model may appear to set out a process to be followed. In fact, however, the model displays the reasoning process of the audit superimposed on the stages of the audit process. 11

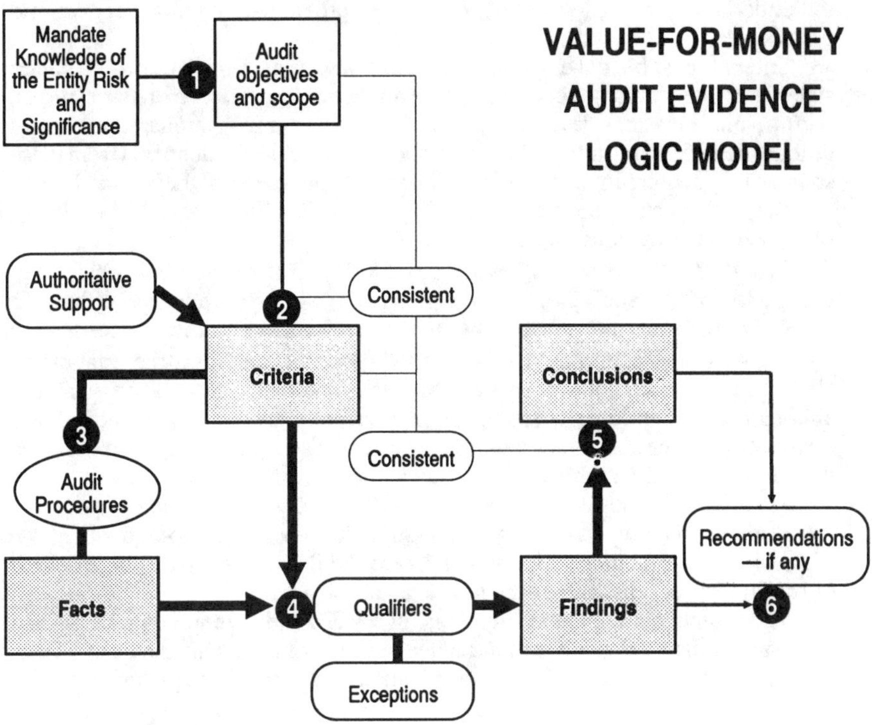

2 CICA Public Sector Auditing Statement 4, *Value-for-Money Auditing Standards*, para. .37.

12 The Value-for-Money Audit Evidence Logic Model can be described as follows:

- *DECISION POINT 1* — The audit objectives and scope are determined during the planning phase of the audit, based upon factors such as the audit mandate, knowledge gained about the entity, an analysis of audit risk and an assessment of matters of potential significance.

  Evidence — The audit objectives are based upon the audit mandate. The audit scope, which must be clearly linked to the objectives, is defined in terms of the entity to be audited and the time period subject to audit. In planning the audit, the auditor should carry out an analysis that assesses a number of factors: knowledge obtained about the entity in previous audits, information and statistical data available at the time the audit is being planned, risks that the entity might face, matters of significance to the entity and to the audit, and other relevant information. This analysis defines the objectives and scope of the audit. The basis for decisions made on the objectives and scope should be documented in the working papers.

- *DECISION POINT 2* — Audit criteria are developed, consistent with the audit objectives and scope previously established.

  Evidence — Criteria may range from general to specific. Criteria at a general level are broad statements of acceptable and reasonable management practices. Specific criteria are derived from general criteria and are more closely related to the entity's governing legislation, objectives, programs, systems, controls and practices.[3]

  Criteria may be developed from such sources as: legislation and policy statements; standards of good practice developed by professions or associations; performance measures developed within the entity or among similar entities; and criteria identified in similar value-for-money audits. Criteria identified from these sources may require interpretation and modification to ensure their suitability.[4]

  The authoritative sources supporting the audit criteria should be clearly identified in the working papers.

- *DECISION POINT 3* — Following the development of the audit objectives, scope and criteria, audit programs are prepared detailing the audit procedures to be performed. Facts are gathered through the performance of these procedures.

  Evidence — Facts should be supported by proof; they must be established "beyond reasonable doubt". This means that strong evidence must be obtained, although in some cases a statement in a report may be based upon direct observation by the auditor, or it may be a generally accepted truth, circumstances that do not normally require additional evidence.

  As is the case with the legal standard of "proof beyond a reasonable doubt", there are no precise guidelines to measure the degree of proof required — professional judgment is still required. There should be, however, a high degree of probability, or reasonable certainty, to establish a fact.

  An example of "factual information" in a VFM audit report could be the use of financial data provided by an auditee system. This system may have been tested, perhaps as part of a financial audit, and found to provide reliable

---

[3] CICA Public Sector Auditing Guideline 1, *Planning Value-for-Money Audits*, March, 1990, para. .30.

[4] *Ibid.*, para. .32.

information. It is rarely possible, however, to carry out an examination of all the transactions or data processed by a system. Instead, reliance must be placed on controls in the system and the degree of risk must be assessed in a manner similar to that employed in a financial statement audit, with a high level of confidence that the audit risk is very low. This is one situation in a VFM audit where applying financial audit testing methods will be appropriate.

- *DECISION POINT 4* — The facts are assessed in relation to the criteria.The auditor's knowledge about the entity helps to establish the audit findings. During this assessment, consistency with the audit objectives, scope and criteria must be maintained — findings that are not relevant to these must be reevaluated. Significance also plays an important role in this assessment.

  In stating the audit finding, the auditor must assess the degree of confidence in the audit finding, based upon the strength of the evidence. The assessment must be clearly reflected in the wording of the finding, with suitable qualifying words used to express the degree of certainty of the finding. As part of this critical assessment, exceptions to the finding may have been established — if significant, these should be included in the description of the finding.

  Evidence — The findings should be supported by persuasive evidence. The degree of credibility attached to the finding can vary from virtual certainty to a degree of certainty equivalent to that associated with an audit conclusion, which is persuasive. An analysis of cause and effect often forms part of the assessment process through which findings are determined. Adequate documentation of the evidence supporting the finding and the degree of support that has been established should be recorded in the working papers.

- *DECISION POINT 5* — The findings provide the basis for the conclusions, with consideration also being given to whether the broad criteria established for the audit have been met. Consistency with the objectives and scope of the audit must also be maintained. In reaching these conclusions, the degree of support provided by the evidence must be evaluated. This assessment must be clearly reflected in the wording of the conclusions, with suitable qualifications if necessary.

  Evidence — The conclusions should be supported by persuasive evidence. In determining whether there is sufficient appropriate evidence to support the conclusions, the auditor must ensure that the evidence obtained is comprehensive enough to match the broad criteria. Adequate documentation of the evidence supporting the conclusion and the degree of support that has been established should be recorded in the working papers.

- *DECISION POINT 6* — In many cases, value-for-money audit reports include recommendations, although these are not mandatory. If a cause and effect analysis has been carried out, the recommendations are often designed to address the causes that have been identified, or to correct specific problems identified in the audit findings and conclusions.

  Evidence — Documentation should include, where appropriate, evidence that a recommendation will have the desired remedial effect on the problem it is intended to address, and is justified in relation to the cost of its implementation.

This logic model pulls together many of the ideas presented in this study. As such, 13
it provides a conceptual model to guide VFM auditors. It illustrates that the development of audit findings and conclusions is a logical process, dependent for its

success on the auditor obtaining persuasive evidence to support the content of the auditor's report.

14 The evidence concepts recommended in this study may not have the precision and mathematical appeal of those associated with financial statement audits. Because of the substantial use of professional judgment in arriving at conclusions based on audit evidence, value-for-money auditors must build their arguments carefully, based on sound evidence that will withstand challenge. The auditor's report must present persuasive arguments, suitably qualified when necessary, which accurately describe the degree of support provided by the evidence that has been obtained.

ATTRIBUTES OF AUDIT EVIDENCE

15 The terms "sufficient" and "appropriate" are not specifically defined in the *Value-for-Money Auditing Standards*. The CICA *Handbook*, however, contains definitions of these terms that are also appropriate for value-for-money auditing. The Handbook describes sufficiency as *the measure of the quantity of audit evidence obtained*. Appropriateness is described *as the measure of its quality*.[5]

16 The sufficiency, or quantity, of evidence can represent either:

- the volume of evidence that has been obtained, e.g., the number of individual facts that have been gathered or the number of items that have been examined;
- the completeness of the evidence, e.g., whether the facts and findings are sufficient to permit an adequate comparison with the audit criteria and thereby provide persuasive support for the audit conclusions.

17 The appropriateness, or quality, of audit evidence relates to its *relevance* and *reliability*. To be relevant, audit evidence must assist the auditor in achieving the audit objective. The reliability of audit evidence depends on its *nature* and *source*.[6]

GAO Field Standards

18 The GAO *Field Standards for Performance Audits* provide further descriptions of the terms sufficient, relevant and reliable (although they use the term "competent", which is defined as valid and reliable).

19 In commenting on the "tests of evidence", the Field Work Standards state that:

> a. Sufficiency: Sufficiency is the presence of enough factual and convincing evidence to support the auditors' findings, conclusions, and any recommendations. Determining the sufficiency of evidence requires judgment. When appropriate, statistical methods may be used to establish sufficiency.
>
> b. Relevance: Relevance refers to the relationship of evidence to its use. The information used to prove or disprove an issue is relevant if it has a logical, sensible relationship to that issue. Information that does not is irrelevant and therefore should not be included as evidence.

---

5 CICA *Handbook*, Section 5300, Audit Evidence, para .09.

6 *Ibid.* para. .15.

c. Competence: To be competent, evidence should be valid and reliable. In evaluating the competence of evidence, the auditors should carefully consider whether reasons exist to doubt its validity or completeness. If so, the auditors should obtain additional evidence or reflect the situation in the report.[7]

APPLICATION OF THE VALUE-FOR-MONEY AUDIT EVIDENCE STANDARD

The VFM evidence standard states that: 20

> Sufficient appropriate audit evidence should be obtained to afford a reasonable basis to support the content of the auditor's report.[8]

Additional guidance on application has been provided in the paragraphs that follow the recommended standard. This guidance is based directly on similar wording contained in Handbook Section 5300 on Audit Evidence.

Risk

The *Value-for-Money Auditing Standards* suggest that: 21

> In determining the sufficiency and appropriateness of evidence, the auditor is guided by the need to minimize the risk of reporting erroneous findings or inappropriate conclusions.[9]

This establishes a key principle related to the evaluation of evidence. The auditor should assess audit risk, i.e., the likelihood that there may be errors in the audit report. This introduces the need for a way to measure the probability of reporting erroneous findings or inappropriate conclusions. 22

There are three stages in a VFM audit where the assessment of risk plays a particularly important part. 23

- In setting the objectives and scope of a VFM audit, the auditor needs to consider the components of audit risk.
- In determining the audit procedures to be carried out, the auditor must consider the nature, extent and availability of evidence that is required to reduce audit risk to an acceptable level, i.e., to minimize "erroneous findings or inappropriate conclusions".
- In reporting findings and conclusions, the auditor must assess the degree of support provided by the evidence obtained and relate this to the earlier risk assessment. If high risk factors have been identified, the auditor must ensure that the quantity and quality of evidence match the degree of risk.

Significance and risk are usually assessed together. If both significance and risk are judged to be high in a particular area, the evidence required to support findings and conclusions in that area must be evaluated carefully to ensure that it provides solid support. 24

---

7 GAO *Government Auditing Standards*, p. 6-17.

8 CICA Public Sector Auditing Statement 4, *Value-for-Money Auditing Standards*, para. .31.

9 *Ibid.*, para. .32.

25 The assessment of risk in a VFM audit, and the related concept of significance play an important role in the evaluation of evidence. A detailed exploration of these concepts is not within the terms of reference of this study. The importance of these topics in a VFM audit suggests, however, that they merit further research.

Interrelationship of Sufficiency and Appropriateness

26 Another key principle is provided in the next paragraph of the *Value-for-Money Auditing Standards:*

> The sufficiency and appropriateness of evidence are interrelated concepts and refer to the quantity and quality of evidence. The decision as to whether a sufficient quantity of evidence has been obtained will be influenced by its quality.[10]

27 High quality evidence can reduce the need for a large quantity of evidence; a large quantity of evidence can sometimes, but not always, be persuasive, even though individual pieces of evidence are not of high quality.

28 This interrelationship between the sufficiency and appropriateness of evidence means that in practice they cannot be discussed as separate attributes to be measured. The auditor cannot expect to determine whether, first, enough evidence has been obtained, and then, second, whether the right quality of evidence has been obtained. In evaluating evidence, the quantity and quality of the evidence must be considered together.

Reliability

29 Another evidence principle is that the reliability of evidence varies with its source and type:

> Generally, evidence obtained directly by the auditor (for example, through observation or analysis) is more reliable than information obtained indirectly, and documentary evidence is more reliable than oral evidence.[11]

30 This VFM guideline on reliability suggests that the most reliable evidence is usually that obtained directly by the auditor; evidence indirectly obtained from the auditee or from third parties is less reliable. In addition, it suggests that written evidence in the form of a report or confirmation should be more reliable than a statement made during an interview.

31 This guidance is taken directly from paragraph .20 of Section 5300 of the Handbook, which adds that external evidence is more reliable than internal evidence. Although this "hierarchy of reliability" is acknowledged to be generally appropriate for financial statement audits, the Study Group believes that it is less applicable to value-for-money audits.

32 The nature of oral evidence is such that its reliability must be carefully assessed. For example, some comments in an interview that appear to be factual may later prove to be partially or completely inaccurate. Other statements may be ambiguous

---

[10] *Ibid.*, para. .33.

[11] *Ibid.*, para. .34.

and may have been misinterpreted. In addition, opinions may change, and events and circumstances may be perceived differently by different people. Oral evidence differs in this respect from written evidence, which is tangible and not subject to shifts in opinion. Accordingly, the auditor should be aware of the basic characteristics of oral evidence in assessing its reliability.

It is not unusual in a VFM audit, however, for the auditor to obtain documents in the form of correspondence, memos or reports that may contain incomplete, ambiguous or even, in some cases, incorrect information. Interviews, on the other hand, can provide more detailed and complete descriptions, since the interviewer is able to clear up ambiguities or probe areas in depth. This allows the auditor to obtain a thorough understanding of not only the essential facts, but also the environment and constraints that may influence an audit finding. The auditor must, therefore, consider the nature of the evidence in each individual case, rather than regarding written evidence as inherently more reliable than oral. 33

The idea that external evidence is more reliable than internal evidence is generally true in a financial statement audit, and provides the rationale for obtaining written confirmations from customers of outstanding accounts receivable, and from creditors of outstanding debt. In VFM audits, however, the reliability of evidence depends much more on the circumstances of the audit than on a "hierarchy of evidence". For example, little use is made of third party confirmations, since in many areas the most reliable information is available only within the entity being audited. 34

In summary, the auditor must exercise professional judgment in determining whether to accept evidence as reliable, or whether to seek additional confirming evidence. 35

Persuasiveness

The focal point of the audit is the process through which the auditor digests, analyzes, assesses and reassembles the facts, and finally reaches a decision on the finding to be reported. This leads to another important principle: 36

> The auditor may find it necessary to rely on evidence that is persuasive rather than conclusive.[12]

This study has already suggested that evidence supporting audit findings and conclusions will usually not provide conclusive proof. The measurement standard to be applied is persuasiveness. 37

The degree of proof required for findings and conclusions cannot normally be as high as that supporting facts. This is because professional judgment plays a significant role in their determination and the degree of certainty is accordingly lower. 38

This can be compared to the legal standard of proof in a civil case. There, as in VFM audits, the standard of proof varies from case to case, depending upon the strength of the evidence. The standard of proof for findings and conclusions in a VFM 39

---

[12] *Ibid.*, para. .35.

audit is almost always less than "beyond reasonable doubt" but more than the civil evidence standard of "a balance of probabilities". This latter standard represents less conclusive evidence than that required in a VFM audit. It is not enough that a finding or conclusion is based on slightly stronger evidence than that supporting other alternatives. In assessing alternatives, the auditor must be satisfied that there is a clear-cut choice — if there is not, additional evidence must be gathered or further analysis must be carried out.

40 The appropriate basis for assessing findings and conclusions is whether they are supported by persuasive evidence. One technique that is used by some practitioners is the "reasonable person" approach. Through an advisory committee or some other form of challenge, findings and conclusions are tested by asking the question, "What would a reasonable person conclude, based on the evidence presented?"

41 The question of "who is to be persuaded" must also be considered. Initially, it is the auditor who must be convinced. The auditor must be persuaded that the findings and conclusions to be reported are neither erroneous nor inappropriate. The evidence should also be persuasive enough to convince the management of the auditee. It is recognized that this does not always happen, and the auditee response may cause some reconsideration of the position previously reached and the strength of the supporting evidence. Although the auditor is not required to review the findings and conclusions with the auditee, it is prudent to do so, to ensure that all relevant facts are known that could affect the conclusions. Finally, of most importance, the evidence must be convincing enough to persuade the client, the provider of the audit mandate, to whom the audit report is addressed.

42 A final word on *persuasive evidence*. The Study Group has focused attention on the evaluation of evidence and the conversion of facts to findings, a process by which an auditor is persuaded that there is sufficient appropriate audit evidence. The auditing standard on evidence, however, refers to *affording support to the content of the auditor's report*. This is the most important test for the VFM auditor. The auditor may be satisfied that persuasive evidence has been gathered. The challenge is to write a report that persuades the reader as to the soundness of the findings and conclusions.

43 This emphasizes the importance of writing audit reports that are logical, clear and persuasive, but at the same time using words and phrases that reflect reality. The auditor should not suggest that the audit findings and conclusions are factual or virtually certain, if the degree of available proof is considerably short of certainty.

Corroboration

44 There is a final principle that is also very important:

> ...the auditor normally seeks corroborating evidence from different sources or of a different nature in making assessments and forming conclusions.[13]

45 A single type of evidence is less persuasive than if several types of corroborating evidence are obtained. For example, if the only evidence consists of information obtained in an interview, this may be less persuasive than if the auditor can obtain

---

[13] *Ibid.*, para. .35.

confirmation by direct observation, or can obtain written confirmation. In general, a greater degree of credibility is provided by cumulative evidence from different sources and of different types than the degree of credibility attached to individual items of evidence: the sum is greater than the parts.

It must be emphasized, however, that the need for corroborating evidence from 46
different sources or of a different nature is a matter of professional judgment. In some cases, evidence from a single source can be very persuasive. For example, certain facts, such as the existence of a written policy, may be firmly established through documentation, making additional confirmation through oral evidence or analysis unnecessary. Direct observation by the auditor of a system or process in operation can also provide persuasive evidence. In summary, therefore, the auditor must carefully assess each individual situation before deciding on the need for corroborating evidence.

A further caution relates to evidence that is contradictory rather than 47
corroborative. If this happens, more evidence must be obtained. If this additional evidence clearly establishes that the contradiction is a unique exception, then the proposed finding can be retained. For example, the auditor may find that a criterion has generally been met, even though individual instances of failure to meet the criterion have been found (it is assumed that the individual instances are not significant in size or in number).

If evidence is not available to resolve the contradiction, the finding should be 48
reassessed. Under no circumstances should the auditor proceed without resolving a significant contradiction.

Chapter 6

TYPES AND SOURCES OF EVIDENCE

INTRODUCTION

Evidence is not confined to auditing. The types of evidence needed by auditors are also common to many other fields. For example, Estey's *Report of the Inquiry into the Collapse of the CCB and Northland Bank* supports its conclusions by summarizing the testimonial evidence it received, the documentary evidence it examined and the analysis that was carried out based on this evidence.[1] 1

The Study Group has already noted the common features of legal and audit evidence, such as the restricted use of hearsay evidence. In legal cases, hearsay evidence is not generally admissible in court, since its accuracy cannot be verified (an exception can be that of an expert, who is permitted to testify on matters not personally observed). Similarly, in a VFM audit, second-hand information (not personally observed) obtained during interviews that cannot be confirmed by the auditor is not usually accepted as audit evidence. 2

Parallels in science, medicine and other fields could also be drawn. The essential point, however, is that, although the types of evidence gathered are similar, each field has established its own principles and "rules" for gathering and evaluating evidence. 3

Many of the terms used to describe evidence in financial statement audits and in VFM audits are the same, which on the surface would suggest that they should be interpreted in the same way. As this study has already concluded, however, these two forms of auditing differ and the techniques for gathering and evaluating evidence also differ in some respects. 4

---

[1] The Honourable Willard Z. Estey, *Report of the Inquiry into the Collapse of the CCB and Northland Bank*, August, 1986.

TYPES AND SOURCES OF VFM AUDIT EVIDENCE

5 There are four types of audit evidence:

- physical;
- documentary;
- oral;
- analytical.

6 These categories correspond closely to those identified by the GAO, which are equally applicable to VFM audits:

> a. Physical evidence: Physical evidence is obtained by direct inspection or observation of (1) activities of people, (2) property, or (3) events. Such evidence may be documented in the form of memoranda summarizing the matters inspected or observed, photographs, charts, maps, or actual samples.
>
> b. Documentary evidence: Documentary evidence consists of created information such as letters, contracts, accounting records, invoices, and management information on performance.
>
> c. Testimonial evidence: Testimonial evidence is obtained from others through statements received in response to inquiries or through interviews. Statements important to the audit should be corroborated when possible with additional evidence. Testimonial evidence also needs to be evaluated from the standpoint of whether the individual may be biased or only have partial knowledge about the area.
>
> d. Analytical evidence: Analytical evidence includes computations, comparisons, reasoning, and separation of information into components.[2]

7 There are three sources of VFM audit evidence:

- *Auditor* — evidence that the auditor originates, including interview notes, analyses, notes on direct observation, etc.
- *Organization* — evidence from the audited organization, including interviews, studies, data and reports.
- *Third parties* — evidence from other parties, including those served by the audited organization and specialists such as actuaries or engineers. Third party evidence may include surveys, confirmations, reports and statistics.

---

2 GAO Government Auditing Standards, p. 6-16/17, para. 58.

The chart shown below links the type of evidence gathered to the methods commonly used to obtain that evidence, and to the documentation required. 8

TYPES, METHODS OF OBTAINING AND DOCUMENTATION OF VFM AUDIT EVIDENCE

TYPES	METHODS OF OBTAINING	DOCUMENTATION
		(recording details of evidence and how it was obtained)
Physical	Inspection or observation of activities, property or events	Summary of matter inspected or observed, including: • notes • photographs • charts • maps • audio/visual
Documentary	Enquiry Surveys	Documents obtained during the audit, including: • management reports on performance • policies and procedures • system descriptions • letters and memos • contracts • studies • confirmations • survey results
Oral	Enquiry Interviews	Summary of information obtained in response to enquiries or through interviews
Analytical	Analysis, through reasoning, reclassification and comparison Computation, the checking of calculations made by the auditee	Summary of analytical data, decisions and conclusions Summary of work done

Physical Evidence

Physical evidence is gathered by observing work activities, examining capital projects, inspecting facilities and similar actions. This type of direct evidence is usually the most persuasive that an auditor can obtain. 9

Documentary Evidence

Documentary evidence is obtained throughout the audit in the form of reports, data, correspondence, and so on. It may be specifically requested by the auditor or may be 10 volunteered by the auditee during interviews or briefings. This type of evidence includes written confirmations obtained from the auditee and third parties.

11 Documentary evidence is usually less reliable than physical evidence (although this depends very much on the circumstances). The source of documentary evidence is also important — in some instances, internal documents may furnish persuasive evidence supporting a finding, but, in other cases, the accuracy of an internal document may be suspect, and corroborative evidence is required.

Oral Evidence

12 This study has already commented on the nature of oral evidence as part of the discussion of the reliability of evidence. Oral evidence plays a much more important role in VFM audits than in most other types of audits. In particular, interviews are a primary means of gathering information and evidence. Interviews differ from inquiries in that they are usually designed to cover a range of topics, and are flexible as to the questions asked and the subject matter covered. Inquiries, which are common to both VFM and financial statement audits, are usually intended to elicit specific information. In a VFM audit, they are often carried out as a follow up to an interview.

13 Information obtained during interviews may often represent very persuasive evidence. Events observed by those being interviewed and their actual experience with respect to the systems and operations being audited often provide information not obtainable from other sources. Explanations provided during interviews are often invaluable — they give the auditor vital information needed in the evaluation of evidence.

14 For important evidence obtained during an interview, it is common practice to obtain written confirmation, particularly if the information will appear in the auditor's report. This ensures that there is agreement on what was said. Depending on the nature and importance of the item, confirmation of oral evidence will also often be obtained through further interviews or from other sources.

15 In summary, oral evidence is particularly important in a VFM audit, but the auditor must be cautious. Uncorroborated statements and statements that are more opinion than fact must be carefully assessed and whenever possible confirmed before they can be accepted as evidence.

Analytical Evidence

16 Analytical evidence is obtained by using professional judgment to evaluate physical, documentary and oral evidence. Initially, the auditor reclassifies and assesses the detailed information obtained during the audit examination. Analytical evidence also includes an assessment of the degree of proof supporting facts, the degree of support that facts provide for findings and conclusions, and, overall, the degree of support for the content of the auditor's report.

MANAGEMENT FEEDBACK

17 An important aspect of obtaining evidence is the feedback received from management at various stages of the audit. Practices vary, but many VFM auditors

have set up a formal process to discuss facts with the management of the auditee before using them to develop audit findings. This process does not provide proof that the fact is correct, but guards against incomplete or inaccurate information obtained by the auditor during the audit. It also provides management with an opportunity to provide additional relevant information that may not have come to the attention of the auditor.

The auditor may also wish to hold briefings with management or provide draft 18
copies of audit reports for comment, providing a vehicle for management feedback. This may lead to a better knowledge of the issues. In some instances, it may also result in a modified finding or conclusion based on new evidence that has been obtained as a result of management's observations.

The facts, findings and conclusions in the auditor's report must be supported by 19
sufficient appropriate audit evidence, but it is usually prudent to also obtain management feedback before preparing a final audit report.

Chapter 7

EVALUATING EVIDENCE

INTRODUCTION

The evaluation of evidence has already been identified as a key part of a VFM audit. 1
Much of the discussion in Chapter 5 on sufficient appropriate audit evidence revolves around the evaluation of evidence and considers factors that influence the evaluation. The rigour with which the evaluation of evidence is carried out, and the judgment and professionalism that are applied, will ultimately determine the success or failure of the audit.

It is not necessary to repeat the discussion on evaluating evidence presented in 2
previous chapters. There are some aspects of evaluating evidence, however, that have not been discussed.

RELEVANCE TO AUDIT OBJECTIVES, SCOPE AND CRITERIA

In evaluating evidence, the auditor may determine that certain findings, although 3
significant in relation to the overall operations of the audit entity, are either:

- not relevant to the stated objectives of the audit;
- not within the defined scope of the audit;
- not relevant to any of the criteria established for the audit (in some cases, this may lead to a reassessment of the completeness and appropriateness of the wording of the criteria, if in all other respects the finding seems to be relevant to the audit objectives).

Significant findings outside the objectives, scope and criteria of the audit may be 4
reported separately from the report on the audit performed. This can be done through a separate report, or by some other means, depending upon the significance and potential effects of the finding.

A fundamental principle of auditing is that the auditor reports against the 5
objectives, scope and criteria that have been set for the audit — the audit procedures are designed with this in mind. This is why relevance has been identified as an essential attribute of evidence.

MATCHING CONCLUSIONS AND SUPPORTING EVIDENCE

6 After the facts and findings in a VFM audit have been determined, there are two additional considerations:

- The findings must be evaluated to arrive at a conclusion on whether the broad audit criteria established for the audit have been met. In making this decision, it is important for the auditor to ensure that the findings have the same breadth as these criteria, so that a valid conclusion can be reached. The auditor cannot conclude on a broadly worded criterion based on findings that do not have similarly broad coverage.
- Having reached a conclusion on whether the criteria have been met, the auditor must ensure that the wording of the conclusion accurately reflects the strength of the evidence that supports it.

COST OF OBTAINING EVIDENCE

7 The cost of obtaining evidence is always a major consideration in a value-for-money audit. The auditor faces continuous choices in deciding how to allocate limited audit resources. This exerts pressure on the auditor to gather evidence as efficiently as possible and to avoid getting more evidence than is necessary to provide adequate support for findings and conclusions.

8 The cost of obtaining evidence cannot be allowed, however, to supersede the evidence standard that requires sufficient appropriate evidence to support the content of the auditor's report. In simple terms, if the auditor does not have persuasive evidence to support a finding or conclusion, it should not be reported.

9 Several different evidence sources generally provide stronger evidence than a single source. Thus, it may be more cost-effective to try a different audit technique rather than to commit extensive resources to the tabulation and analysis of detailed data.

FACTORS TO CONSIDER IN EVALUATING EVIDENCE

10 There are a number of factors to be considered in evaluating evidence. The following list is not necessarily all-inclusive, but covers some of the main factors to be considered:

- *Relevant* — Is the evidence relevant to the audit objectives, scope and criteria? If not, it cannot provide support for the audit findings and conclusions.
- *Representative* — Is the evidence representative, and therefore capable of supporting an observation on performance generally, or is it an isolated instance?
- *Consistent* — Is the evidence (particularly oral evidence) subject to change, and is it confirmable?
- *Authoritative* — Is there adequate authority for the policies and practices of the organization?
- *Credible* — Has the evidence been obtained from a source that is reliable? If not, this assessment will lead to the need for corroborative evidence.
- *Objective* — Has the information been obtained from a source likely to be unbiased? If not, corroborative evidence will be needed.
- *Complete* — Is the evidence complete, or is there additional evidence that might provide a more complete picture?

- *Timely* — Is the evidence on which the findings and conclusions are based timely and likely still to be valid as support for the findings and conclusions?
- *Internal check* — Has the evidence been confirmed by internal verification procedures, or is it obtained from information systems that have adequate controls?
- *Contradictory evidence* — Has any contradictory evidence been obtained? If so, has it been satisfactorily explained and any anomalies resolved?

LOGICAL FALLACIES

There is another important aspect of evaluating evidence. Theories of logic suggest the means by which rational conclusions are reached, based on evidence. This study has used these theories to develop logic models applicable to VFM audit evidence. But what if the conclusions are not "rational"? 11

The theory of logic also includes the concept of *logical fallacies* — ways in which invalid conclusions can be reached through faulty reasoning. VFM auditors should be aware of the types of unsound arguments that fall within the description of logical fallacies. Listed below are some of these *logical fallacies*; types of fallacies with particular applicability to VFM auditing have been selected for discussion. 12

Fallacies are arguments that can seem persuasive despite being unsound. The danger lies in the fact that the argument is not obviously incorrect; without careful examination, a fallacious argument can appear to be reasonable. 13

The phrases describing the fallacies which are quoted below in italics appear to have gained general acceptance, although the fallacies themselves have been classified in many different ways.[1] Fallacies can be grouped under five headings: 14

- missing facts;
- irrelevant facts;
- defective facts;
- unwarranted assumptions;
- ambiguities in the report.

Missing Facts

One logical fallacy involving missing facts is known as *begging the question.* This refers to the practice of advancing grounds as support for a conclusion that are really a re-phrasing of the claim they are intended to support. Arguments of this type are also referred to as "circular arguments", since they have no firm foundation in fact. 15

VFM auditors can avoid this type of fallacy by ensuring that examples included in the auditor's report are sufficient to support the conclusions based on those examples. For example, care should be taken not to use only symptoms of a problem as examples supporting a conclusion, without also providing illustrations of the cause of the problem. 16

---

[1] The fallacies listed in this section are selected from those described in Irving M. Copi's *Introduction to Logic*, Fifth Edition, Macmillan Publishing Co., 1978, and Toulmin, Rieke and Janik's *An Introduction to Reasoning*, Second Edition, Macmillan Publishing Co., 1984.

Irrelevant Facts

17 Another type of fallacy is a fallacious *appeal to authority*. This happens when an acknowledged authority is cited, but in an inappropriate way.

18 This can occur in a VFM audit if an expert is quoted in an area outside of that person's field of expertise; when an expert opinion is not supported by adequate evidence; or, as sometimes happens, when an expert's opinion is disputed by another expert. In each of these instances, the contention that a conclusion is valid because "our expert agrees with it" would be a fallacious argument.

19 A second example of irrelevant facts is an *argument from ignorance*. This occurs when a conclusion is reached based on the absence of contrary evidence. In a VFM audit, there must be confirming evidence, not just a lack of contradictory evidence.

20 A third example of irrelevant facts can occur if outdated information is used. Care must be taken in a VFM audit to ensure that statistical and other information used as evidence is sufficiently current to be relevant to the conclusions drawn from it.

Defective Facts

21 A fairly common fallacy, and one that is particularly important to the evaluation of VFM audit evidence, is that of *hasty generalization*, or jumping to conclusions.

22 VFM auditors can guard against this fallacy by ensuring that samples selected are sufficient to allow a valid conclusion to be reached. Samples drawn must be large enough (sufficient) and representative of the population (typical). This applies to both statistical and judgmental samples. Statistical sampling, properly applied, is used by auditors to reduce the problem of hasty generalization by confining the risk within known parameters. Judgmental samples must also be sufficient and typical.

23 This fallacy can also occur outside a sampling context. In some cases, the auditor can encounter a situation or circumstance during the audit that may or may not be typical. Great care must be taken not to generalize from isolated examples. Objectivity is of particular importance. If auditors prejudge conclusions, they may believe there is support for a finding or that an occurrence is typical, when in fact it is not. The effects of unintended bias can be far-reaching.

24 Responses to the survey questionnaire would seem to indicate that some respondents are prepared to reach conclusions based on random samples that are not intended to be representative. This practice can lead to "hasty generalization".

Unwarranted Assumptions

25 There are several varieties of this fallacy, including:

- *False cause* — this fallacy can arise through an auditor concluding that because event A precedes event B, it must have been the cause. This is not necessarily true.
- *False analogy* — this fallacy demonstrates the potential danger of using analogies to provide support for a conclusion. In some cases, the analogy may not be appropriate, resulting in inadequate support for the conclusion.

Ambiguities in the Report

The use of imprecise or vague language in the auditor's report can result in fallacies such as *equivocation*. This occurs when a word or phrase is used with more than one meaning in the same argument, thereby producing what seems to be, but is not, a logical conclusion. 26

VFM auditors can avoid this type of fallacy by choosing words to convey the exact meaning that is intended, and using these words consistently throughout the report. Careful editing to remove vague references or confusing sentence structure can also help to guard against ambiguities in reporting. 27

Chapter 8

EVIDENCE UNDER DIFFERENT VALUE-FOR-MONEY AUDIT MANDATES

INTRODUCTION

There is considerable diversity in the way in which VFM audits are performed. One reason for this diversity is the different mandates under which VFM auditors operate. In this chapter, the effect of different mandates on VFM audit evidence will be considered. The mandates to be discussed include: 1

- federal and provincial legislative audits;
- special examinations of federal Crown corporations (including a discussion of the use of an attestation audit approach based on management assertions);
- municipal and non-legislated audits;
- internal audits; and
- mandates outside Canada.

FEDERAL AND PROVINCIAL LEGISLATIVE AUDITS

Federal and provincial auditors and auditors-general have generally similar VFM audit mandates, although there is some variation in reporting requirements. As might be expected, however, the way in which they conduct VFM audits varies with the type of entity, the nature of the area subject to audit, and with the different audit office structures and methodologies employed.[1] 2

Similar approaches to evidence have been adopted. The types and sources of evidence and the techniques used to gather evidence appear to be generally consistent and vary more with the type of audit than with the audit mandate. 3

---

[1] A different type of mandate is that of the Office of the Auditor General of Alberta. Alberta's Auditor General Act, in Section 19(2)(d), requires calling attention to every case in which the Auditor General has observed that "accounting systems and management control systems, including those systems designed to ensure economy and efficiency, that relate to revenue, disbursements, the preservation or use of assets or the determination of liabilities were not in existence, were inadequate or had not been complied with". This approach suggests a greater concentration on system assessment than occurs in other VFM audits.

4 Accordingly, the Study Group has concluded that the concepts of evidence discussed in this research study are suitable for legislative auditors practising VFM auditing in Canada.

SPECIAL EXAMINATIONS OF FEDERAL CROWN CORPORATIONS

5 The legislation establishing a special examination regime for federal Crown corporations differs substantially from that which created the federal and provincial legislative mandates. Unique features of the special examination mandate include the following.

- The purpose of the special examination is to determine if the financial and management control and information systems and management practices of the corporation are maintained in a manner that provides reasonable assurance that:
  a) the assets of the corporation and each subsidiary are safeguarded and controlled; and
  b) the financial, human and physical resources of the corporation and each subsidiary are managed economically and efficiently and the operations of the corporation and each subsidiary are carried out effectively.[2]
- The special examiner must provide an opinion on whether there is reasonable assurance that there are no significant deficiencies in the systems and practices examined.[3]

6 Special examination mandates differ from legislative VFM mandates in several ways:

- the phrase *reasonable assurance* in the overall opinion describes the degree of certainty that the auditor (special examiner) is expected to achieve as a result of the special examination. This differs significantly from those legislative audit mandates that refer to reporting instances of lack of due regard for economy and efficiency.
- the special examiner must provide an opinion on *significant deficiencies* in the systems and practices examined. Other VFM mandates do not have this mandatory requirement and the wording of conclusions varies substantially.

7 Together, these requirements have led to special examination reports that are different from those of other types of VFM audits. The opinions provided cover the entire entity reported on, and contain the specific opinions required by the Financial Administration Act.

---

2 Financial Administration Act, Part X Crown Corporations, Part XII, Section 138 (2)(a) and (c).

3 *Ibid.*, Section 143 (7)(a).

The Office of the Auditor General of Canada (OAG), which performs the majority of the special examinations, has set out the main steps in conducting a special examination in the following chart.[4] 8

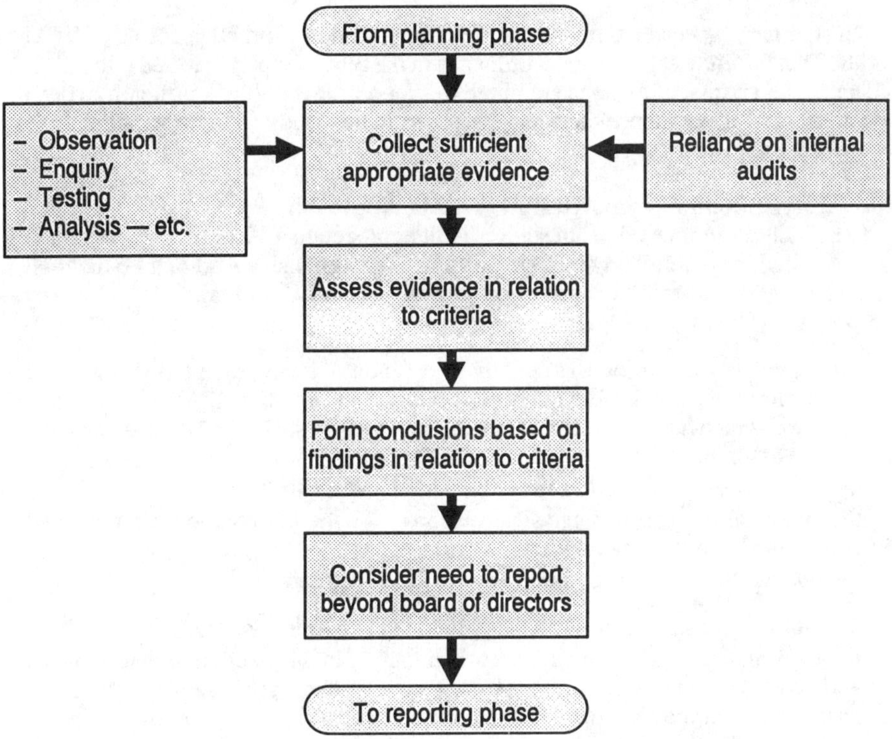

The OAG approach stresses the need for an evaluation of the corporation's achievement of its control objectives.[5] This approach includes an assessment of risk and the identification and review of key systems and practices. 9

---

4 *A Framework for the Conduct of Special Examinations in Crown Corporations*, the Office of the Auditor General of Canada, 1987, p. 38.

5 *Ibid.*, pp. 14, 37 and 39 describe this approach as follows:

> The aim should be to concentrate the examination on those areas where deficiencies could be significant. In this context, a *significant* deficiency is a deficiency in systems and practices (e.g., in their design, their operation or even their existence) of such a nature that it puts at material risk the achievement of one or more of the specific control objectives. ...It is important to recall that the corporation itself is required to have reasonable assurance that the statutory control objectives are achieved. Therefore, in gathering evidence, the examiner should obtain such information as is available regarding the extent to which the corporation's key control objectives are achieved.
>
> As well as being a starting point for the examination, this type of information can be a potential source of evidence on:
>
> - whether the related operational and support systems and practices are satisfactory; and
> - whether the corporation has information systems that contribute to providing it with the reasonable assurance it is supposed to have.

10 The OAG approach also refers to the special examiner's obligation to use the results of internal audits to the extent practicable. If the examiner relies on internal audit work, "the examiner bears responsibility for the validity of all evidence upon which the opinion is based.".[6]

11 In summary, special examinations are quite different from other forms of VFM audits. That difference, however, is primarily in the type of report required rather than the nature and extent of evidence required to support the report. It has therefore been concluded that the evidence concepts discussed in this study are appropriate for use by special examiners.

Special Examination — an Attestation Audit Approach

12 A documented example of an attestation audit approach to a VFM audit is contained in an Applied Research Study by the Canadian Comprehensive Auditing Foundation (CCAF) on the special examination of the Canada Mortgage and Housing Corporation (CMHC).[7]

13 This special examination was essentially an audit of the representations prepared by the Corporation, which were intended to support its assertion that the CMHC had systems and practices in place that are maintained in such a manner to provide reasonable assurance that:

- the assets of the Corporation are safeguarded and controlled;
- the financial, human and physical resources of the Corporation are managed economically and efficiently; and
- the operations of the Corporation are carried out effectively.[8]

14 The audit approach adopted was implemented at two levels:

- the Corporation made individual representations in 14 functional/sectoral areas and provided documentation supporting each of the representations. The audit team reviewed the documentation and assessed the key systems and practices supporting the information on which the representations were based.
- the Corporation made a global representation (incorporating the 12 attributes of effectiveness developed by the CCAF) that related to the detailed representations that had been made. The Special Examiner provided the following opinion on this representation:

> In my opinion, based on the criteria established for the evaluation of these systems, there is reasonable assurance that there are no significant deficiencies in the systems and practices examined.

---

6 *Ibid.*, p. 39.

7 *Reporting and Auditing Effectiveness, The Experience of Canada Mortgage and Housing Corporation*, CCAF Applied Research Series, 1990.

8 *Ibid.*, Appendix 2, p. 19.

> Further, in my opinion, based on the agreed upon framework, the Corporate Representation as at June 30, 1989 reports on, in a reasonable and complete way, the most important aspects of the effectiveness of the Corporation and the Corporation has the information, systems and practices in place to support the statements contained therein.[9]

As reported in the Applied Research Report: 15

> The process used by the audit team ...is similar to the traditional audit approach in a financial audit. The approach was systems based, focusing on key systems and practices as defined in the functional/sectoral representation documents.[10]

The types of evidence obtained and the techniques used in this audit appear to be similar to those used in other special examinations, except that much of the support for the representations was prepared by the Corporation, not the audit team. The audit team tested the relevance, reliability and completeness of the data and assessed the systems that prepared the data. In addition, the audit assessed whether there were significant deficiencies in the systems and practices examined, and concluded that there were not. 16

In summary, the CCAF's Applied Research Report appears to confirm this study's earlier conclusion that, although special examination reports are different from those of other VFM audits, the evidence concepts in this study can be applied to special examinations, including those that attest to management representations. 17

MUNICIPAL AND NON-LEGISLATED AUDITS

Value-for-money audits are performed by municipal auditors in many of Canada's larger cities and regional municipalities. Some are governed by legislation and others by municipal bylaws. 18

There are major differences in mandates and audit approach. In general, however, the evidence concepts that were judged to be appropriate for legislative auditors also appear to be relevant to VFM audits performed by municipal auditors. 19

There are similarly many different types of value-for-money audits performed in hospitals, non-profit organizations, and other entities that do not have a legislated requirement for a VFM audit. Again, the types and sources of evidence and the concepts related to evaluating evidence that are described elsewhere in this Study would appear to be appropriate. 20

INTERNAL AUDITS

Many public sector internal auditors have value-for-money audit mandates. These mandates and the types of audits carried out range from audits that are organized in a similar fashion to those of external auditors to internal audits that include a limited number of VFM objectives and procedures. 21

---

9 *Ibid.*, Appendix 3, p. 23.

10 *Ibid.*, Appendix 4, p. 25.

22 External auditors may choose to use internal audit reports as evidence in their audits. As noted in Public Sector Auditing Guideline 1,

> If evidence is to be obtained from other audits or studies, the auditor would assess: the relevance of the objectives, scope and criteria to the planned value-for-money audit; whether the work was conducted in accordance with value-for-money auditing standards; the competence and independence of the auditor or reviewer; and the reliability of the conclusions of the audit or study.[11]

23 As is the case with other non-legislated audits, the concepts in this study would appear to be applicable to most internal audits.

MANDATES OUTSIDE CANADA

24 Performance audits undertaken by the General Accounting Office in the United States and Value-for-Money audits carried out by the National Audit Office in the UK (under legislation enacted in 1983) operate under different mandates from those found in Canada. Nevertheless, guidance provided to auditors in those countries on evidence parallels that provided to Canadian VFM auditors (for example, this study has quoted from the GAO Field Standards for Performance Audits, which are relevant to practice in Canada).

25 Value-for-money auditing is also carried out in many other countries, under a wide variety of mandates. Audits in Sweden, for example, are focused on an assessment of the effectiveness of programs, and use techniques suitable for that purpose.[12] The mandate of the Federal Court of Audit in Germany also includes performance audits.[13] Some countries, such as Australia and New Zealand, have adopted practices that are similar to those in Canada, and comparable evidence techniques are employed.

26 The International Organisation of Supreme Audit Institutions (INTOSAI) has issued auditing standards that include standards for performance auditing.[14] The evidence standard is generally similar to that of the GAO field audit evidence standard, as is the guidance that accompanies the standard.

27 Overall, practices in other countries have evolved under many differing mandates, and reflect local requirements and circumstances. Audit techniques vary accordingly, but these countries appear to have adopted generally similar approaches to gathering and evaluating audit evidence.

---

[11] CICA Public Sector Auditing Guideline 1, *Planning Value-for-Money Audits*, para.34.

[12] Swedish National Audit Bureau, *System-Oriented Effectiveness Audit — Concept & Implementation*, 1985.

[13] Federal Court of Audit of the Federal Republic of Germany, *Information Booklet*, 1988.

[14] INTOSAI *Auditing Standards*, June 1989.

Chapter 9

SURVEY RESPONSES

INTRODUCTION

An exhaustive discussion of all of the types of evidence and techniques for gathering evidence would be a mammoth task. Because of the diversity of mandates, practices and preferences, it is not practical to try to identify and assess all of the different approaches that have been tried in all of the audits that have been conducted. In VFM auditing, it is probably fair to say that no two audits are identical. In fact, very few VFM audits follow a standard pattern, a factor which, as this study has already concluded, differentiates VFM from financial attest audits. 1

Observations on current practice are, however, an important part of this study. To obtain the views of practitioners on preferred practices for gathering and evaluating VFM audit evidence, a questionnaire was sent to selected practitioners asking them to answer a wide range of questions on techniques currently employed (a summary of their responses is contained in Appendix F). The views expressed are not intended to be a statistically valid sample of current practice — instead, they are a sampling of opinion from individual practitioners. 2

This chapter analyzes the responses to the survey questionnaire. It should be noted, however, that not all of the questions in the survey are included in this analysis. The Study Group believes that the answers to some of the questions speak for themselves and do not require further comment. It also suggests using caution in assessing the responses. The answers provided by respondents suggest that some questions were interpreted in different ways. Some unusual patterns of responses may be accounted for by these differences in interpretation. 3

The Study Group believes that the responses of practitioners to the survey are generally consistent with the positions put forward in this study. In a few cases, however, statements by some of the respondents have raised issues that concern the Study Group. These concerns are set out as part of the analysis of responses. 4

NATURE AND EXTENT OF EVIDENCE

The questionnaire asked respondents to rate the importance of various factors in determining the nature and extent of evidence required, solicited views on when 5 evidence is required and on the need for quality control, and asked respondents to rate the extent of their use of various techniques to gather evidence.

Importance of Various Factors in Determining the Nature and Extent of Evidence Required

6 Respondents believe that important findings and conclusions require solid evidence. Three factors were clearly considered to be the most important in determining the quality and quantity of evidence required:

- the significance of the audit finding;
- the degree of certainty expressed by the audit conclusion; and
- the form of report or nature of audit assurance to be given.

7 This study also regards these as important factors and has stressed their effect on the quantity and quality of audit evidence required.

8 Audit risk, environment, effectiveness of internal control and cost were all rated as fairly important (although some respondents were unsure whether "internal control" might mean financial controls or management controls). Gathering the least support were cooperativeness of the auditee and receptiveness to the audit (although four placed it among their top two in priority), and time constraints.

When Evidence is Required

9 Most respondents agree that evidence is required to support facts and conclusions. There is more doubt about the need to have evidence supporting recommendations, and a clear majority do not require evidence for management responses (although several respondents stated that they ensure the responses are "reasonable", and take action if they are not).

10 Most respondents suggest that some form of support for audit criteria is required, but vary in their description of the kind of evidence needed. A few suggest that only client concurrence with the criteria is needed. The Study Group agrees that criteria require supporting evidence, and have proposed that the authoritative sources that provide the support should be clearly identified.

Quality Control

11 Most respondents have some form of quality control. Advisory committees, audit office quality control functions and second party reviews are commonly used, and some of the smaller offices presently without some of these controls indicate that they are planning to implement them.

12 Rather surprisingly, however, the most frequently cited control is the auditee organization. Some respondents appear to view agreement by the management of the auditee as a major source of evidence; they suggest that the need to assess the sufficiency and appropriateness of evidence only arises if the auditee challenges the audit findings. The Study Group does not believe that the nature and extent of evidence should depend upon the reaction of the auditee. In its view, if persuasive evidence for a finding or conclusion has not been obtained, the finding or conclusion should not be reported.

Techniques Used to Gather Evidence

The most frequently chosen techniques are: 13

- oral enquiry of persons inside the organization being audited; and
- the inspection of records and documents.

The support for oral enquiry as a technique confirms the vital importance of interviews as a primary source of VFM audit evidence.

Techniques frequently used, but given less support, include: 14

- observation and documentation of processes and procedures;
- visits to work sites;
- comparison with other organizations;
- analysis and evaluation of internal control (mixed results in the responses reflect uncertainty about the VFM meaning of "internal control").

The following are also used and are listed in order of support: 15

- reliance on specialists;
- oral enquiry outside the organization being audited;
- checking calculations;
- written enquiry inside the client being audited;
- inspection of physical assets;
- reliance on internal control or program evaluation;
- written enquiry outside the client being audited.

TESTING AND INTERNAL CONTROL

The questionnaire solicited views of practitioners on their use of testing techniques and on the evaluation of internal controls, topics that occupy much of the CICA *Handbook* discussion of audit evidence. 16

Statistical and Judgmental Sampling

Although sampling is widely used as a technique for obtaining audit evidence, practice appears to vary considerably. Respondents report that they use statistical sampling much less frequently than judgmental sampling. Some of the comments received on this question raise a concern that the "samples" selected may in fact not be representative of the total population. If this is the case, they are unlikely to support a conclusion on the population as a whole. Instead, they may represent an intentional search for examples of problems. 17

The Study Group believes that such a procedure should not be described as sampling, since the examples selected are not "typical". These are unlikely to represent "sufficient appropriate audit evidence" to support conclusions on the total population. 18

Evaluation of Internal Controls

Many respondents (76%) agree that the concepts of "reliance on internal control" and "compliance testing" are relevant to VFM audits. There is general agreement, however, on a reduced role for the testing of controls and reliance on internal controls in a VFM audit, as compared with the key role it plays in a financial statement audit. Respondents suggest that few formal evaluations of the effectiveness of internal 19 control take place, although control assessments form part of the audit of specific systems.

OPINIONS ABOUT VALUE-FOR-MONEY AUDIT EVIDENCE

20 The questionnaire asked for opinions about evidence as well as for information on current practices. Many of the opinions expressed were fairly predictable, others were unexpected. In a few cases, the variation in opinion was extreme, suggesting that a great divergence of views exists, or that there were different interpretations given to words or phrases in the question, or perhaps both.

21 Several questions dealt with audit objectives, scope, criteria and recommendations:

a) Most respondents agreed that evidence is needed to support decisions on scope and objectives, but many were not sure how "evidence" should be interpreted. There was general support, however, for the view that decisions on scope and objectives are essential elements in planning the audit, and support for these decisions should be documented; for example, comments included, "we need to show why scope and objectives are as selected", and "there should be documented rationale to support decisions on scope and objectives".

b) Most agreed that criteria should be "reasonable", but there was no agreement on what that means. To some, this requires supporting evidence, and they strongly disagree with the statement that, if the auditee agrees with the criteria, they do not require any further support. Others take the opposite view — if the criteria stand up to challenge by the auditee, no evidence is required. This study stresses the need to document authoritative sources that provide support for the audit criteria.

c) Most agreed that support for recommendations is useful, but some noted that recommendations are often general and flow directly from the audit conclusions. Other respondents noted that recommendations are often self evident after identifying the problem; little or no additional evidence is needed.

22 Respondents consider internal audit reports or consultant's reports to be acceptable as evidence, but not as the only source. Before acceptance as supporting evidence, these reports should be subject to critical analysis and review.

23 There was general agreement that several interviews which corroborated each other can provide sufficient evidence — "in some cases, it's the best evidence there is". The Study Group, however, believes that caution must be exercised in the use of oral evidence. As a minimum, corroborative interviews should occur at different levels in an organization. For important issues, supporting evidence of different types and from different sources is usually necessary.

Objectivity of the Auditor

24 Most respondents (70%) disagree with the statement that, "It is much more important to have evidence for a 'positive' finding than for a 'negative' one", but 8% agreed and 22% were neutral.

In commenting on the statement "If the auditee does not object to a finding, then no further evidence is required", opinions were split, with 48% in agreement, 42% disagreeing and 10% neutral. 25

Some of the responses to these two statements raise the issue of the auditor's objectivity in gathering evidence. For example, if the sufficiency and appropriateness of evidence depend on whether a finding is positive or negative, rather than on the significance of the finding, or whether the auditee objects to the finding, the auditor may be subject to challenge on the basis that the evidence gathered is based on how the auditor perceives the findings will be received, rather than providing persuasive, objective support for all findings. 26

The Study Group believes that auditor independence is important and can be maintained by adopting an objective approach to evaluating evidence. 27

A contentious and somewhat surprising response was received to the statement, "It is always preferable to have very strong evidence, but if I feel that I have an important finding, I'll report the matter based on relatively weak evidence." The majority (57%) agree with this statement, but 25% of the respondents disagree, 15% of them strongly. 28

Comments on this question raise additional concerns. Some respondents suggest that a description of the lack of evidence will be satisfactory. Other respondents place great reliance on the auditee's reaction to the finding. If the reaction is negative, they will look for more evidence or drop the finding; if the finding is accepted, they will not seek more evidence. 29

This again raises the question of the auditor's objectivity, since the auditee may have hidden motives for accepting or disputing findings. The Study Group believes that the auditee's acceptance or rejection of findings cannot justify reporting findings based on weak evidence. 30

Chapter 10

CONCLUSIONS AND CHALLENGES

CONCLUSIONS OF THIS STUDY

In gathering evidence, the value-for-money auditor faces much different decisions than those encountered by the traditional auditor of financial statements. 1

The financial statement audit examination is focused on obtaining evidence to support the auditor's opinion on the statements. Concepts of audit testing, risk assessment and materiality have emerged to help the auditor decide how much and what kind of evidence is needed to be able to express this opinion. 2

Value-for-money auditors report the results of their audits in a different manner. They provide a series of conclusions, often related to individual audit projects, rather than a single conclusion. These conclusions are based largely on the application of qualitative rather than quantitative measures. As a result, value-for-money auditors have a much different task in determining the sufficiency (how much) and appropriateness (what kind) of evidence they need to support their conclusions. The challenge is to translate the evidence standard of *sufficient appropriate audit evidence* into something more precise and definable that is useful to practitioners, corresponding to the extensive methodology, standards and guidelines that have evolved in financial statement auditing to give concrete meaning to "sufficient" and "appropriate". 3

This study proposes an approach to evidence that is based on concepts of logic and reasoning. Value-for-money audit procedures must be directed towards obtaining persuasive evidence to support the findings and conclusions in the auditor's report. The importance of evaluating the strength of the evidence obtained has been stressed throughout this study. A distinction has been made between the evidence required to support each of the following: 4

- *facts* — proof beyond reasonable doubt;
- *findings* — the evidence should be compelling enough to provide strong support, but will rarely attain the degree of probability that can be labelled as proof;
- *conclusions* — the evidence must be persuasive, which is a judgmental term, but one that appears to be generally understood. Conclusions are derived from findings — no additional evidence is needed.

5 The Study Group believes that the concepts in this study provide the framework that will allow value-for-money auditors to determine the sufficient appropriate audit evidence they need to support the content of their auditor's reports. This study has not attempted to prescribe specific methods of applying these concepts, nor has it prescribed specific techniques that value-for-money auditors should apply in obtaining and evaluating evidence.

6 Much work needs to be done before specific guidance can be provided. This study has already noted the diversity of mandates and current practices. The suitability of the approaches that have been suggested in this study must be assessed by practitioners in different types of audits, using different styles of reporting. Practitioners are urged to test new approaches to gathering and evaluating the sufficient appropriate audit evidence needed to support their reports, and thereby help to promote the continuing development of value-for-money auditing.

CHALLENGES ARISING FROM THIS STUDY

7 The Study Group believes that practitioners face a number of challenges related to VFM audit evidence.

Standards and Guidelines on Value-for-Money Audit Evidence

8 Practitioners need guidance on value-for-money audit evidence. The type of guidance needed is roughly equivalent to the "rules of evidence" in the field of jurisprudence.

9 The courts, in the absence of mathematical probability concepts (that are believed to be inappropriate for reaching legal decisions), have developed rules of evidence that define the type of evidence that is admissible in court and the manner in which it must be presented and evaluated. This is not to suggest that the same rules should apply to VFM auditing, but rather that there is a need for some basic ground rules to promote consistency in VFM audit practices.

10 PSAAC should undertake to provide guidance to value-for-money auditors in the form of Standards and/or Guidelines, but only after allowing sufficient time for a thorough evaluation of the issues, time for some of the ideas to have been tested in practice, and after an assessment of the readiness of practitioners to accept the proposed concepts.

11 The Study Group proposes that the guidance should include:

An interpretation of the meaning to be given to the term "sufficient and appropriate audit evidence".

This study has suggested a number of ways in which this can be done. As has been stressed throughout, the VFM auditor needs to understand how to interpret this VFM evidence standard. At present, Section 5300 of the CICA *Handbook* on Audit Evidence is often used as a reference source, but this Section has limited applicability to VFM auditing. By providing guidance, PSAAC can promote better accountability and consistency in practice, and enhance the integrity and credibility of VFM auditing.

Guidance on the application of risk and significance concepts to value-for-money auditing.

Risk and significance are closely related concepts and cannot be assessed separately. The assessment of risk in particular has a significant effect on the process of gathering and evaluating evidence. The Study Group believes that a conceptual approach to VFM audit evidence cannot be fully developed until the related risk and significance concepts have also been addressed. In particular, VFM auditors must have a clear understanding of suitable sampling techniques and circumstances where they may, or may not, be appropriate.

Guidance on appropriate techniques for obtaining and evaluating evidence.

The Study Group has cautioned that some of the evidence concepts borrowed from financial statement auditing, particularly the "hierarchy of evidence" concept, are not fully applicable to VFM audits. In these and other areas (such as interviewing, an essential technique used in most VFM audits), guidance by PSAAC would assist practitioners.

In each of these areas of challenge, further research and experimentation must 12
take place and the views of practitioners should be sought on desirable and necessary practices. The Study Group believes, however, that meeting these challenges will contribute greatly to the continued growth and acceptance of value-for-money auditing.

Appendix A

LITERATURE REVIEW

The review of literature as part of this research study began with a review of reference sources directly related to audit evidence and value-for-money auditing. These had been identified by PSAAC as primary reference sources and included: 1

- CICA Public Sector Auditing Statement 4, *Value-for-Money Auditing Standards,* March 1988
- CICA Public Sector Auditing Guideline 1, *Planning Value-for-Money Audits,* March 1990
- CICA *Handbook*, Section 5300 — Audit Evidence
- United States General Accounting Office, *Government Auditing Standards*, 1988
- CICA Research Study, *Extent of Audit Testing*, 1980
- Canadian Comprehensive Auditing Foundation (CCAF) Professional Development Course, *Evidence in Comprehensive Auditing*
- Audit manuals of practitioners involved in value-for-money auditing

Other sources related to audit evidence include the works that are the traditional foundations of auditing theory, and the research studies and other CICA publications which have dealt with evidence-related concepts such as risk and materiality. Of particular interest was the research study, Professional Judgment in Financial Reporting, which assessed the environmental factors and characteristics of human behaviour that influence the application of professional judgment.[1] 2

In order to provide a broader perspective in studying concepts of evidence, a number of other avenues were explored. One area of obvious interest is that of legal evidence, on which a great deal has been written. Other material on evidence is contained in the articles, guidelines and audit manuals produced in other countries, particularly material related to performance auditing in the United States and value-for-money auditing in the United Kingdom. 3

Another area of interest is in the developing disciplines of forensic accounting and auditing, and environmental auditing. Forensic and environmental auditing, 4

---

[1] Gibbins, Michael and Mason, Alister K., *Professional Judgment in Financial Reporting,* CICA Research Study, 1988.

although similar in some respects to VFM auditing, have apparently not yet generated literature on evidence concepts. In addition, forensic work is closely identified with the court system and concepts of legal evidence, so that existing legal principles rather than newly developed audit principles apply. Program evaluation literature was also reviewed, since there are similarities to VFM audits and the growth of program evaluation in Canada in many ways parallels that of VFM auditing.

5 Finally, there is a wide body of academic literature and research in areas of interest to this study. Some is related to evidence supporting an auditor's opinion on financial statements. Other reference sources are less obvious, but have proven to be of considerable interest. Literature on concepts of logic, reasoning and probability, all of which enter into the process of evaluating VFM audit evidence, have proven to be of particular interest and relevance.

6 Literature reviewed in the course of this research study is listed in the bibliography. In summary, the literature that proved to be of the most interest and represents the basic foundation for this study falls into three areas:

- basic auditing concepts, and the standards and guidance provided to implement these concepts;
- legal evidence concepts;
- logic and reasoning concepts, particularly as they relate to evidence in support of conclusions.

7 The review of literature has lead to several conclusions:

1. Literature on audit evidence is primarily focused on the evidence needed to support an auditor's opinion on a set of financial statements. This would seem to provide a useful basis for developing parallel guidance on VFM audit evidence. Specifically, Section 5300 of the *Handbook* provides extensive guidance on the sufficiency and appropriateness of evidence, and on methods of obtaining evidence, both subjects of direct interest to this study. Further, the wording of the *Handbook* and PSAAC evidence standards is virtually identical, suggesting that there are close parallels.

   In fact, however, the apparent similarities did not prove to be as great as might have been supposed. There are significant differences in financial statement and VFM audits. A major difference is that mathematical probability plays an important role in assessing the sufficiency and appropriateness of evidence in a financial statement audit. This concept cannot be applied in the same way to VFM audits.

2. Literature dealing with logic concepts ranges from observations by Aristotle about the way in which conclusions are established, to present day philosophical theories and propositions about logic and reasoning. Applications of a formalized reasoning process have been applied successfully in several non-scientific as well as scientific fields. For example, concepts of statistical sampling are widely used in financial statement auditing.

   Many, however, question whether "scientific" logic can be applied universally. They point out that in the field of jurisprudence, for example, assessing the probability of guilt is a key element in criminal court cases. The introduction of mathematical probability concepts, however, has been resisted, and "rules of evidence" have been developed using quite different concepts. Generally, proponents of a "non-scientific" approach have concentrated on developing alternative concepts that explain how logical conclusions can be reached without applying mathematical techniques.

3. As an alternative to the mathematical probability model that has been successfully applied to the audit of financial statements, the study has looked at logic models based on other concepts. In particular, the views of Stephen Toulmin, as set out in *The Uses of Argument*,[2] and subsequently in *An Introduction to Reasoning*,[3] have been used in developing a model to demonstrate the VFM audit evidence process.

---

2 Toulmin, Stephen, *The Uses of Argument*, Cambridge University Press, 1958.

3 Toulmin, Stephen; Rieke, Richard; Janik, Allan; *An Introduction to Reasoning*, Second Edition, Macmillan Publishing Co., 1984.

Appendix B

VALUE-FOR-MONEY AUDIT EVIDENCE SURVEY QUESTIONNAIRE

NATURE AND EXTENT OF EVIDENCE

1. How important is each of the following in determining the nature and extent of evidence gathered in a value-for-money (VFM) audit?
   a) significance of the finding?
   b) effectiveness of internal control?
   c) current environment in which the auditee operates?
   d) cooperativeness and receptiveness of auditee to audit and audit findings?
   e) risk of auditee's failure to meet audit criteria?
   f) the degree of certainty expressed by the audit conclusion?
   g) the form of report or nature of audit assurance to be given?
   h) cost of obtaining evidence?
   i) time constraints?
2. Refer to items (a) to (i) of question 1 and indicate in order of priority the three that you consider to be the most important.
3. In your view, must evidence be gathered in respect of each of the following, if they appear in the auditor's report:
   a) audit criteria?
   b) assertions of fact?
   c) the auditor's conclusions or opinions?
   d) recommendations, including their appropriateness and cost-effectiveness?
   e) management's responses?
4. To whom must you demonstrate the sufficiency and appropriateness of your evidence:
   a) one or more members of your Office who are not directly involved in the audit?

   b) an advisory or supervisory committee assembled specifically to deal with your audit?
   c) an Office quality control function?
   d) the auditee organization?
   e) only yourself?

5. In financial auditing it is generally accepted that the reliability of evidence differs according to whether its source was the auditor him/herself, the auditee organization, or a party outside of the auditee organization. Do you feel the same view applies to value-for-money (VFM) auditing?
6. For each of the techniques of obtaining evidence listed below, indicate the extent to which you have used them in VFM audits.
   a) Inspection of records or documents.
   b) Inspection of physical assets.
   c) Visits to work sites.
   d) Observation and documentation of processes or procedures.
   e) Oral enquiry of persons inside the organization being audited.
   f) Written enquiry or confirmation addressed to persons inside the organization being audited.
   g) Oral enquiry of persons outside the organization being audited.
   h) Written enquiry or confirmation addressed to persons outside the organization being audited.
   i) Checking the arithmetic accuracy of data provided by the auditee or performing independent calculations.
   j) Analysis of components and interrelationships contained in financial and other information.
   k) Comparison of the auditee with other similar organizations.
   l) Analysis and evaluation of the system of internal control.
   m) Reliance on internal audit or program evaluation.
   n) Reliance on the work of a specialist.
7. Refer to the techniques listed in items (a) to (n) of question 6 and indicate in order of priority the three that you consider to be the most commonly used.
8. Audit criteria sometimes are stated broadly. Before you set out to obtain evidence, do you define with greater precision what characteristics will, if found, indicate that a broadly stated audit criterion has or has not been met?
9. Do you require that audit criteria be supported by evidence in the same sense that audit findings and/or conclusions are required to be supported by evidence? If evidence is required, what kind of evidence would normally be needed?
10. Is the nature and extent of the evidence you gather governed by policies of your Office or largely by your personal judgment?

11. Indicate below the frequency with which you use sampling techniques:
    a) statistical sampling
    b) judgmental sampling

    Please indicate the circumstances under which you find each of these approaches to sampling to be most appropriate.

TESTING AND INTERNAL CONTROL

The terms "compliance procedures" and "substantive procedures" are often used in connection with obtaining audit evidence. Compliance procedures are used to gain a sufficient degree of assurance whether internal controls are operating effectively, whereas substantive procedures are used to gain evidence as to the validity of data and auditee representations.

12. Do you consider the concepts of "reliance on internal control" and "compliance testing" relevant to value-for-money auditing?
13. If you consider that these concepts of reliance on internal control and compliance testing are relevant, please answer the following questions. If not, skip to question 14.
    a) Do you evaluate the effectiveness of internal control for all major systems?
    b) Do you assess the effectiveness of the overall system of internal control applicable to the area subject to audit rather than evaluate the controls in each separate system?
14. When you use statistical data obtained from sources internal to the auditee, do you perform any tests to ensure its reliability?

REACTION TO STATEMENTS ABOUT VALUE-FOR-MONEY AUDIT EVIDENCE

15. For each of the following statements indicate the extent to which you agree or disagree. Where possible, please provide comments or examples to illustrate your views.
    a) It is much more important to have evidence for a "positive" finding than for a "negative" one.
    b) If the auditee does not object to a finding, then no further evidence is required.
    c) Statements made by auditee officials in interviews cannot by themselves constitute sufficient and appropriate evidence, although they may lead to other sources of evidence.
    d) Where I have engaged a consultant to provide an expert opinion and there is a disagreement between "my expert" and "the auditee's expert," I usually favour the view of my consultant.
    e) If the auditee has an internal audit report or consultant's report that supports the point I want to make, I usually accept the report as supporting evidence.

f) In a VFM audit report we may want to say that systems or procedures are not in place. However, it is very difficult to gather evidence which proves that something doesn't exist.

g) When dealing with "soft" issues you can't demand the same rigour in the evidence as you can when dealing with "hard" issues.

h) It's always preferable to have very strong evidence, but if I feel that I have an important finding I'll report the matter based on relatively weak evidence.

i) When I have a very sensitive issue, I demand evidence that is absolutely convincing.

j) Usually, several types of evidence are needed, but sometimes a piece of evidence is so convincing that I don't require any other corroboration.

k) In general, if I'm reporting on specific deficiencies rather than giving an overall opinion, I don't require as much evidence.

l) If I'm giving an overall opinion, I only need evidence to support any particular facts that I choose to cite in the report, not evidence that the opinion itself is accurate.

m) If, for whatever reason, I think my report is likely to receive an unusually high degree of attention, I demand very convincing evidence of my findings.

n) Oral representations given by two or more individuals, if they corroborate one another, are acceptable evidence.

o) At the outset of an examination my approach does not vary whether I expect to find that the audit criterion has been met or not met. I just plan to gather evidence that will lead me to a correct evaluation, one way or the other.

p) When I'm reporting on a system deficiency, I think that evidence of a compliance deficiency is enough — I don't insist on seeing that a problem has occurred as a result of the deficiency.

q) In some audit areas, I know I can't expect evidence that will convince everyone of my views, so I don't waste resources going after really strong evidence.

r) I always ensure that I have some supporting evidence, even for those items in the report that I consider to be relatively minor.

s) If I have the auditee's agreement that the audit criteria I plan to use are suitable, I don't require any further support for them.

t) Where I have made a recommendation in my report, I feel I must have evidence to support the recommendation, such as evidence to show that the course of action I am suggesting will address the problem, will have the desired remedial effect, and is justified in view of its cost of implementation.

u) Even if the evidence is not particularly strong, the more pieces of evidence I have that point me to the same conclusion, the more comfortable I feel.

v) I think that the opinion of an outside expert is just about the best evidence I can hope to obtain.

w) It doesn't make any difference to me whether I see original documents; these days copies are just as good.

x) I don't demand that I get statements made during interviews subsequently confirmed in writing.

y) I don't need evidence to support my decisions on scope and objectives during the planning phase of the audit; the term evidence just applies to information supporting the contents of the final report.

z) In value for money auditing each case is different, therefore, it is impossible to give anything other than very general guidance about the nature and extent of evidence needed.

EVIDENCE REQUIREMENTS IN SPECIFIC SITUATIONS

16. Financial attest auditing has developed the concept of assertions. The following questions apply the concept to VFM auditing. Note that for our purposes it is irrelevant whether the assertion originates with management or with the auditor.

For each of the following assertions which might appear in an audit report, comment on the nature and extent of supporting evidence you would require as an auditor. Each example is intended to illustrate a particular type of assertion. These types have been noted in square brackets.

Your reply could include the kinds of audit techniques you would apply (such as those listed in question 6), the types of expertise you would employ, the types of documents or data you would obtain, the method of sampling you might apply, the size of samples that you would choose, etc. Comment also on any special problems or considerations you would foresee in gathering that evidence.

a) During an audit of human resource management in a large department you conclude that most job descriptions in the department are outdated. [Assertion about a characteristic of a large population]

b) During an audit of a program which provides financial contributions to organizations carrying out approved projects you conclude that no procedures exist to ensure that money is advanced to recipient organizations only as and when needed. [Assertion about a characteristic of a system]

c) During an audit of information provided to a governing body you conclude that certain reports do not contain appropriate measures of past performance. [Assertion about the characteristics of a document]

d) In reporting on the audit of a major capital project you state that Project Alpha was undertaken at a planned cost of $ 10,000,000 even though prior studies performed by independent consultants at the request of management had projected the benefits to be only $ 7,000,000. Moreover, the actual cost turned out to be $ 12,000,000. [Assertion about the amount of costs and benefits]

e) In reporting on an audit of clerical productivity you conclude that the operation of the claim verification unit in the department is carried out efficiently. In forming this conclusion you have relied upon the work of internal audit. [Assertion about efficiency]

f) In reporting the findings of a follow-up on a previous audit report you state that management has formulated a plan to address your concerns about deficiencies in the accounts receivable system and that work is under way to implement the plan. You state that management's action should rectify the problem. [Assertion about a future event]

FURTHER RESEARCH AND GUIDANCE

17. Have you encountered situations where you would have liked more authoritative guidance on the nature and extent of evidence required? If so, please describe the circumstances.

Appendix C

PSAAC STATEMENTS AND GUIDELINES RELATED TO EVIDENCE

PUBLIC SECTOR AUDITING STATEMENT 4, *Value-for-Money Auditing Standards*

.31 *Sufficient appropriate audit evidence should be obtained to afford a reasonable basis to support the content of the auditor's report.*

.32 In determining the sufficiency and appropriateness of evidence, the auditor is guided by the need to minimize the risk of reporting erroneous findings or inappropriate conclusions.

.33 The sufficiency and appropriateness of evidence are interrelated concepts and refer to the quantity and quality of evidence. The decision as to whether a sufficient quantity of evidence has been obtained will be influenced by its quality.

.34 Generally, evidence obtained directly by the auditor (for example, through observation or analysis) is more reliable than information obtained indirectly, and documentary evidence is more reliable than oral evidence.

.35 The auditor may find it necessary to rely on evidence that is persuasive rather than conclusive. Thus, the auditor normally seeks corroborating evidence from different sources or of a different nature in making assessments and forming conclusions.

Reporting Standard

.36 There is no standard report in current value-for-money auditing practice that is analogous to the auditor's standard report on financial statements. Value-for-money auditing reports vary between jurisdictions and audits depending on differences in audit mandates, and in the scope and complexity of the particular audit and its findings. Regardless of variations in reporting, there are some fundamental elements that should be included in any value-for-money auditing report. These are set out in the general Reporting Standard below.

.37 *The auditor's report should:*

i) describe the objectives and scope of the audit including any limitations therein;

ii) state that the examination was performed in accordance with the standards recommended in this Statement and accordingly included such tests and other procedures as the auditor considered necessary in the circumstances;

iii) identify the criteria and describe the findings which form the basis for the auditor's conclusions; and

iv) state the auditor's conclusions.

.38 It is important that the report describe the objectives of the audit examination and what has been audited so that readers can understand and properly interpret the results. The objectives of the audit are based on the audit mandate and should set out clearly the purposes of the particular audit. The scope of the audit is described by identifying the entity, or portion thereof, subject to audit (for example, the corporation, department and/or program); identifying or referring to the matters examined; and describing the time period covered by the audit.

.39 Any limitations in scope and the reasons therefor should be described in the audit report. A scope limitation occurs, for example, when the auditor is unable to audit key organizational units or systems or to perform necessary audit procedures due to factors beyond the auditor's control. The scope of the audit can also be limited by the inability to identify or agree on suitable criteria, as discussed in paragraphs .28 and .30. The auditor would consider whether it is appropriate to comment in the report on the implications of the lack of suitable criteria for the entity being audited.

.40 The general and examination standards set out the professional qualities expected of auditors engaged in value-for-money auditing and basic standards for the conduct of value-for-money audit examinations. Thus, the report should inform readers that the examination was performed in accordance with these standards and that the auditor made judgments as to what tests and other procedures were necessary in the particular circumstances to comply with the standards.

.41 The report should identify the criteria and describe the findings sufficiently to allow readers to understand the basis upon which the auditor formed his or her conclusions. Audit findings arise from an examination of the underlying facts, comparisons with suitable criteria and the auditor's analyses. The criteria upon which the auditor made his or her assessments and formed his or her conclusions may be made apparent in the description of findings or may be set out separately in the report. Alternatively, the auditor may refer the reader to an accessible source. In any case, the criteria should be clearly identifiable.

.42 The report should clearly state the auditor's conclusions. Conclusions should be related to the objectives and scope of the audit and should follow logically from the description of the criteria and findings.

.43 Value-for-money audit reports may also incorporate the auditor's recommendations, as well as management's responses with respect to the matters reported.

PUBLIC SECTOR AUDITING GUIDELINE 1, *Planning Value-for-Money Audits*

.23 Auditability relates to whether an audit can be done. Because the objectives and scope vary from one value-for-money audit to another, the auditor needs to assess whether an audit with the proposed objectives and scope can be conducted. The auditor would consider whether:

— there are relevant approaches, methodologies and criteria available; and

— the information or evidence required is likely to be available and can be obtained efficiently.

.34 When planning a value-for-money audit, it is important that the auditor identify the probable nature, sources and availability of audit evidence required. Factors that should be considered include:

— *The effect of the audit approach.* The nature of evidence needed if the audit is to focus more on processes may differ from that required if the audit focusses to a greater extent on results.

— *The ability to integrate audit work with other audits or studies.* If other audit reports or studies are available, the auditor may choose to use them as evidence in the audit. If the auditor is aware of other planned audits or studies, he or she may choose to coordinate work to be able to rely on their reported results. If evidence is to be obtained from other audits or studies, the auditor would assess: the relevance of the objectives, scope and criteria to the planned value-for-money audit; whether the work was conducted in accordance with value-for-money auditing standards; the competence and independence of the auditor or reviewer; and the reliability of the conclusions of the audit or study. The auditor would also determine the need for corroborating evidence.

— *The effect of the reporting requirements.* The amount of evidence required to form an overall opinion on an entity may be relatively greater than that needed to identify and report deficiencies.

— *The cost of obtaining evidence.* The auditor may not be able to obtain evidence from a particular source at a reasonable cost for the planned timing of the audit. In such circumstances, the auditor would assess the possibility of obtaining other appropriate evidence on a timely basis.

Audit Plan

.35 Results of audit planning would be reflected in an audit plan. The audit plan documents key planning information and decisions such as:

— the auditor's understanding of the entity;

— the audit objectives;

— the scope of the audit (i.e., the entity or portion thereof, the matters and the time period subject to audit);

— the planned criteria;

— the probable nature, sources and availability of evidence;

— the resources required;
— the work schedule; and
— the reporting requirements and the timing of the report.

Inclusion of this information in the audit plan provides evidence of compliance with the value-for-money auditing standard on planning.

Appendix D

CICA HANDBOOK SECTION 5300 AUDIT EVIDENCE

TABLE OF CONTENTS — PARAGRAPH

INTRODUCTION AND DEFINITION

.01 Examination standard (iii) (see GENERALLY ACCEPTED AUDITING STANDARDS, Section 5100) states:

> *Sufficient appropriate audit evidence should be obtained, by such means as inspection, observation, enquiry, confirmation, computation and analysis, to afford a reasonable basis to support the content of the report.*

.02 Audit evidence consists of the source documents and accounting records underlying the financial statements and all other information which is pertinent to the auditor's examination. The accounting records, of themselves, do not provide sufficient appropriate audit evidence.

.03 This Section provides guidance in general terms as to the attributes of audit evidence and the manner in which the auditor obtains and evaluates such evidence. While the auditor is concerned with audit evidence in all phases of his audit, this Section deals primarily with such evidence obtained by performing compliance and substantive procedures.

.04 The principal distinction between compliance procedures and substantive procedures is that compliance procedures are used to gain a sufficient degree of assurance whether the prescribed internal controls are operating effectively, whereas substantive procedures are used to gain evidence as to the validity of the data produced by the accounting system. Although the objectives of compliance and substantive procedures are different, both use the same methods of obtaining evidence (see paragraphs 5300.22-.35) and the concepts of sufficiency and appropriateness (see paragraphs 5300.09-.21) also apply to both.

NECESSITY FOR PERFORMING SUBSTANTIVE AUDITING PROCEDURES

.05 It is important to recognize the interrelationship between examination standard (ii) and examination standard (iii). Examination standard (ii) requires an appropriately organized study and evaluation of those internal controls on which the auditor subsequently relies in determining the nature, extent and timing of auditing procedures. Where the auditor has relied on internal control, such reliance and substantive auditing procedures must together provide the assurance he seeks to support the content of his report. Where the auditor has not relied on internal control, such assurance must be provided by substantive auditing procedures more extensive than those which would have been applied if internal control had been relied on. Such procedures may also differ as to their nature and/or timing.

.06 Although the existence of an effective system of internal control reduces the probability of error and fraud, it does not eliminate the possibility that they might have occurred. Because of this and other inherent limitations, such as management overriding an otherwise effective control, the auditor's evaluation of internal control cannot by itself provide him with sufficient evidence that the financial statements are free of material misstatement. Accordingly, the auditor will need to perform some substantive auditing procedures. This is so even where there is a well-designed internal control system and the compliance procedures indicate the controls within it have operated effectively throughout the period of reliance.

.07 One inherent limitation of internal controls is that they tend to be directed at regularly recurring transaction streams, and not at unusual transactions. It follows that in performing his substantive auditing procedures, the auditor needs to recognize the possibility of unusual transactions, which may not be subject to the usual internal controls.

.08 *The auditor should perform substantive auditing procedures. This is so even when the internal control system is well-designed and compliance procedures indicate that the controls within it have operated effectively throughout the period of reliance.* [JAN 1978]

SUFFICIENCY AND APPROPRIATENESS OF EVIDENCE

.09 The concepts of sufficiency and appropriateness are interrelated. As used in examination standard (iii), sufficiency is the measure of the quantity of audit evidence obtained and appropriateness is the measure of its quality. The decision as to whether a sufficient quantity of evidence has been obtained will be influenced by its quality. Normally, the auditor finds it necessary to rely on evidence that is persuasive rather than conclusive. Thus, he frequently seeks evidence from different sources or of a different nature to support the same assertion.

.10 When performing substantive procedures the auditor's judgment as to what is sufficient appropriate audit evidence is influenced by such factors as:

a) materiality;

b) inherent risk and control risk considerations;

c) the experience gained during previous audit examinations as to the reliability of the client's records and representations;

d) the persuasiveness of the evidence; and

e) error or fraud found while performing his auditing procedures.

When performing compliance procedures, the auditor would consider the above factors, where applicable, and the particular factors described in INTERNAL CONTROL, paragraphs 5220.16-.21.

Sufficiency

.11 The auditor does not normally examine all available information but forms his conclusions on an entire set of data by examining only a part of it. This procedure is commonly referred to as testing.

.12 The reasons for examining only part of the data to gain reasonable assurance as to the reliability of the entire set of data, and therefore accepting some uncertainty in the results of audit tests, include:

a) the auditor is not seeking absolute certainty;

b) evidence obtained from one source, corroborated by evidence obtained from another source, will normally provide increased assurance;

c) examining all data may still not provide absolute certainty, as for example, where there are certain unrecorded transactions; and

d) the cost of examining every entry in the accounting records and all supporting evidence would generally be uneconomic.

.13 Tests fall into two basic categories:

a) specific item tests whereby the auditor examines individual items which he considers should be examined because of their size, nature or method of recording. For example, in selecting accounts receivable for confirmation, the auditor may select all those over a certain monetary amount and all overdue accounts;

b) representative item tests whereby the auditor's objective is to examine an unbiased selection of items. For example, the auditor may make a representative selection of personnel records for the purpose of testing that changes in payroll rates have been properly authorized.

The auditor may combine both categories of testing as for example,when he selects for examination all items over a certain monetary amount and a further group of representative items.

.14 The determination of an appropriate sample on a representative basis may be made using either statistical or non-statistical methods. Whether statistical or non-statistical methods are used, their common purpose is to enable the auditor to reach a conclusion about an entire set of data by examining only a part of it.

Statistical sampling methods allow the auditor to express in mathematical terms the uncertainty he is willing to accept and the conclusions of his test. The use of statistical methods does not eliminate the need for the auditor to exercise his judgment. For example, he has to determine the degree of audit risk he is willing to accept and make a judgment as to materiality.

Appropriateness

.15 The appropriateness, or quality, of audit evidence relates to its relevance and reliability. To be relevant, audit evidence must assist the auditor in achieving his audit objective. The reliability of audit evidence depends on its nature and source.

.16 The auditor is concerned with the following assertions with respect to internal control:

Existence	— that it exists;
Effectiveness	— that it operates effectively;
Continuity	— that it has so operated throughout the period of intended reliance.

The auditor seeks evidence with respect to these assertions primarily through the performance of compliance procedures (see INTERNAL CONTROL, paragraphs 5220.11-.21).

.17 Financial statement items embody the following assertions:

Existence	— that an asset or a liability of the enterprise exists at a given date;
Occurrence	— that a transaction took place which pertains to the enterprise;
Completeness	— that there are no unrecorded assets, liabilities or transactions;
Ownership	— that an asset is owned by the enterprise at a given date;
Valuation	— that an asset or liability is recorded at an appropriate carrying value;
Measurement	— that a revenue or expense transaction is recorded in the proper amount and allocated to the proper period;
Statement Presentation	— that an item is disclosed in accordance with generally accepted accounting principles (or, where applicable, with another appropriate basis of accounting).

The auditor seeks evidence with respect to these assertions primarily through the performance of substantive procedures. Obtaining evidence relevant to one assertion, for example, existence of inventory, will not compensate for failure to do so for another, for example, its valuation. Some assertions will be virtually self-evident to the auditor, for example, the "valuation" of cash, while others, such as the "completeness" of accounts payable, may require extensive procedures.

.18 In evaluating each internal control on which he intends to rely and in examining each financial statement item, the auditor uses his professional judgment to:

a) identify the relevant underlying assertions;

b) determine the types of evidence available with respect to each assertion; and

c) determine from the available evidence, what constitutes sufficient appropriate evidence with respect to each assertion.

.19 Audit evidence may be classified by its nature — documentary, oral or visual — and by its source — the auditor, the enterprise or third parties. For example:

a) the auditor develops evidence by such means as:
   i) physical inspection of assets;
   ii) recomputation of calculations; and
   iii) observation of the performance of internal control routines.

b) the enterprise produces evidence in the form of:
   i) source documents such as copies of sales invoices;
   ii) accounting records and reports; and
   iii) oral and written representations made by management and employees.

c) third parties provide evidence in the form of:
   i) independent records and reports such as industry statistics;
   ii) source documents such as suppliers invoices; and
   iii) oral and written representations at the request of the auditor, such as accounts receivable confirmations.

.20 Generally, evidence developed by the auditor is more reliable than evidence obtained from the enterprise or third parties, documentary evidence is more reliable than oral evidence and external evidence is more reliable than internal evidence. The auditor may gain increased assurance when audit evidence obtained from different sources or of a different nature is consistent. In these circumstances, he may obtain a cumulative degree of assurance higher than that which he attaches to the individual items of evidence by themselves. Conversely, when audit evidence obtained from one source is inconsistent with that obtained from another, the reliability of each remains in doubt until further procedures have been performed to resolve the inconsistency.

.21 *The auditor should evaluate all the evidence he has obtained and assess its sufficiency and appropriateness. He should consider evidence supporting and evidence refuting an assertion and should be alert for evidence supporting one assertion but inconsistent with that supporting another.* [JAN 1978]

METHODS OF OBTAINING EVIDENCE

.22 The auditor obtains evidence by the performance of a combination of the auditing techniques described in examination standard (iii) — inspection, observation, enquiry, confirmation, computation and analysis. These techniques apply to computerized accounting records although the method of application may differ from that used in other systems.

Inspection

.23 Inspection consists of looking at records and documents or at assets having physical substance. It encompasses techniques of varying degrees of thoroughness such as examining, perusing, reading, reviewing, scanning, scrutinizing and vouching.

.24 Inspection of records and documents provides evidence of varying degrees of reliability depending on their nature and source and the effectiveness of the internal controls over their processing. There are three major categories of documentary evidence, each providing a different degree of reliability to the auditor:

a) Documentary evidence created and held by unrelated third parties

   Documentary evidence created and held by unrelated third parties (such as published records of dividends) is beyond the control of the enterprise and therefore normally constitutes highly reliable evidence.

b) Documentary evidence created by third parties and held by the enterprise

   The majority of the externally-created documents inspected by the auditor will be in the enterprise's possession and will include such items as bank statements, purchase invoices and customers' purchase orders. The reliability of these documents as audit evidence depends primarily on the controls which exist to prevent their being falsified, suppressed or improperly altered by someone within the enterprise.

c) Documentary evidence created and held by the enterprise

   Documents created within an enterprise generally represent less reliable evidence as they may be susceptible to falsification, suppression or improper creation or alteration. Some of these documents may pass through the hands of a third party, for example cheques, while others such as sales invoice copies do not leave the possession of the enterprise. The reliability of these documents as audit evidence depends on the controls which exist to prevent their being falsified, suppressed or improperly created or altered.

Inspection of physical assets provides highly reliable evidence with respect to their existence but not necessarily as to their ownership or value.

Observation

.25 Observation consists of looking at a process or procedure being performed by others. Observation of procedures provides highly reliable evidence as to the manner of their performance at a given point in time but not necessarily as to their performance at other times.

Enquiry and confirmation

.26 Enquiry consists of seeking appropriate information of knowledgeable persons within or outside the enterprise. Enquiries may range from formal written enquiries addressed to third parties to informal oral enquiries addressed to persons within the enterprise. An example of the former is a confirmation enquiry to a bank with respect to deposit or loan balances and an example of the latter is an enquiry of client personnel regarding an internal control procedure. Responses to enquiries may provide the auditor with information which he did not previously possess or may provide him with corroboration. A response from a person within the enterprise does not usually constitute sufficient appropriate audit evidence in itself but requires corroboration. Such corroboration may include making further enquiries from other appropriate sources within the enterprise. Consistent responses from different sources provide an increased degree of assurance.

.27 Confirmation consists of an enquiry, usually written, to corroborate information contained in the accounting records; for example, a confirmation sent to a debtor with respect to an amount receivable from him. Written responses to confirmation requests received directly by the auditor usually provide highly reliable evidence, especially if from unrelated third parties.

.28 The degree of reliability which the auditor attaches to the responses to his enquiries and confirmations will be affected by his judgment as to the objectivity and knowledge of the respondent. When responses to important enquiries and confirmations are not in writing, it is highly desirable that they be documented in the auditor's working papers.

Computation

.29 Computation consists of checking the arithmetical accuracy of source documents and accounting records or of performing independent calculations. Computation provides the auditor with evidence which is highly reliable with respect to arithmetical accuracy.

Analysis

.30 Analysis consists of:

a) identifying the components of a financial statement item or account to determine matters which require investigation; and

b) studying and evaluating the interrelationships between elements of financial and other information, techniques referred to as analytical procedures.

.31 Analytical procedures can be effective in identifying possible financial statement misstatements and may be applied during:

a) the planning phase of the engagement to assist the auditor in identifying unusual or unexpected balances and trends which may affect the nature, extent and timing of the procedures to be performed during the examination;

b) the execution phase of the engagement as a substantive procedure to obtain evidence to verify assertions relating to specific account balances or classes of transactions; and

c) the evaluation phase of the engagement to assist the auditor in assessing the validity of conclusions reached, including the opinion to be expressed on the financial statements as a whole.

.32 Analytical procedures include comparisons of recorded amounts to expectations developed by the auditor. The auditor develops such expectations by considering relationships that are expected to exist based on the auditor's knowledge of the business and industry in which the entity operates. Expectations are developed from a variety of sources including:

a) Financial information for comparable prior periods.

b) Anticipated results — for example, budgets, forecasts, and extrapolations, including extrapolations from interim or annual data.

c) Relationships among elements of financial information within the period.

d) Information regarding the industry in which the client operates.

e) Relationships of financial information with relevant non-financial information.

.33 The decision to use analytical procedures as a substantive procedure is a matter of the auditor's judgment about the expected effectiveness and efficiency of the procedure to achieve a particular audit objective. It may be difficult, however, to achieve certain audit objectives without relying to some extent on analytical procedures. For example, this is often the case in testing for unrecorded transactions. Alternatively, some audit objectives may be difficult or impossible to achieve by relying solely on analytical procedures, for example, when auditing an account balance that is not expected to show a predictable relationship with other operating or financial data. For significant account balances and classes of transactions, it would normally be necessary to use analytical procedures in conjunction with other audit procedures to achieve the audit objectives.

.34 When analytical procedures are used as a substantive procedure or to assist the auditor in assessing the validity of conclusions reached, the expectations developed by the auditor should be precise enough to indicate the possibility of material misstatement, individually or when aggregated with other misstatements. Analytical procedures using expectations developed at a more detailed level have a greater chance of detecting misstatements in excess of a given amount than do broader comparisons. The effectiveness of, and consequently the level of assurance derived from, an analytical procedure depends on, among other things, how thoroughly the auditor considers the factors that affect the amount being audited, the level of detail and reliability of data used to develop the expectation and the method used to convert data into an expectation.

.35 Taking into consideration the intended level of assurance to be derived from an analytical procedure, the auditor would determine whether the amount of difference from the expectation can be accepted without further investigation. The amount of the difference from the expectation that is acceptable without further investigation would, in any event, be less than that which the auditor believes could be material. Unacceptable differences would be investigated further to identify and corroborate the reasons for the differences. Additional procedures which the auditor would perform to corroborate the reasons for the differences include:

a) considering information obtained from management's responses to further enquiries and from other procedures performed; and

b) extending detailed procedures.

TIMING OF SUBSTANTIVE AUDITING PROCEDURES

.36 The auditor may choose to carry out substantive auditing procedures prior to the balance sheet date. When the auditor:

a) performs substantive auditing procedures on the transactions building up to an account balance (as is normally the case with accounts such as sales or fixed assets) for less than the entire period; or

b) obtains evidence supporting an account balance (as is normally the case with accounts such as inventories and depreciation expense) as at a date other than the balance sheet date;

he will need to obtain sufficient assurance that the account balances at the balance sheet date have not been misstated because of incorrect accounting entries and unrecorded transactions in the intervening period. This assurance for the intervening period may be obtained by performing any combination of:

i) compliance procedures to enable him to place substantial reliance on internal control;

ii) substantive tests of transactions; and

iii) other substantive auditing procedures, such as analytical procedures.

.37 When substantial reliance cannot be placed on internal control, the auditor may find it necessary to perform the major portion of his substantive auditing procedures with respect to balance sheet accounts as of the balance sheet date and, with respect to income statement items, up to the balance sheet date.

.38 *When the auditor performs substantive auditing procedures on the transactions building up to an account balance for less than the entire period or obtains evidence supporting an account balance as at a date other than the balance sheet date, he should obtain sufficient assurance that the account balances at the balance sheet date have not been misstated because of incorrect accounting entries and unrecorded transactions in the intervening period.* [JAN 1978]

.39 The auditor needs to consider whether to examine interrelated items at the same time. For example, a purchase may be included in physical inventory, but not recorded in purchases and accounts payable and accordingly, the auditor would normally perform certain auditing procedures on the related trade accounts payable as at the inventory count date.

.40 Events or transactions may occur or new information may become available subsequent to the date of the balance sheet but prior to the date of the auditor's report that require reflection in the financial statements.

.41 *The auditor should consider audit evidence available up to the date of his report to determine whether matters requiring reflection in the financial statements have been identified. After the date of his report, the auditor does not have a continuing responsibility to seek further evidence but should respond to facts or events that come to his attention that may affect the financial statements* (see DATE OF THE AUDITOR'S REPORT, Section 5405 and SUBSEQUENT EVENTS, Section 6550). [MAY 1984]

RELATIONSHIP TO THE REPORTING STANDARDS

.42 The auditor relies on his professional judgment in deciding which procedures will give him sufficient appropriate audit evidence, recognizing that there may be occasions when he will be unable to gain reasonable assurance as to the reliability of the accounting records and the financial statements. The auditor then evaluates the audit evidence obtained to determine the content of his report.

Appendix E

CONCEPTS OF LEGAL EVIDENCE, PROFESSIONAL JUDGMENT, LOGIC AND REASONING

LEGAL EVIDENCE

Chapter 3 outlines some of the similarities (and the differences) between legal evidence and VFM audit evidence. There are other characteristics of legal evidence that also deserve mention. 1

The role of evidence in the legal system and the general nature of the law of evidence should be considered first. Although many of the same principles apply in both criminal and civil cases, the process in a civil case will be briefly outlined. 2

Each side in a dispute presents its own version of what happened to give rise to the dispute. Opposing lawyers present witnesses, documents, exhibits, or anything they can legitimately present, in order to convince the decision-maker — whether judge or jury — that their client's version of the story is correct. The judge or jury meet then to determine what are the "facts", that is, which version of the story will be deemed "correct" for the purposes of the law. In the absence of any procedural error, the decision made will be final and enforceable, and the parties must live with it. 3

The legal system is adversarial. Each party is free to present its case and to define the issues in dispute. After the court has received all the evidence submitted by the parties, each party has the right to make legal arguments based on the evidence. 4

> ...the main purpose of a trial is to establish the facts on which the final decision will be based. A trial should be a search for the truth, but not at any cost. The objective of pursuing the truth must yield to such factors as procedural fairness, time and cost. Thus, the dispute must be decided solely on the evidence legally adduced in the course of the trial. The law of evidence should strike a proper balance between the search for the truth and the other factors. It should also guide and control the trier of fact, the judge or jury, concerning the proper use of admissible evidence in drawing inferences and reaching sound conclusions on questions of fact.[1]

---

[1] Canadian Encyclopedic Digest (Western Edition), Vol II Title 57, *Evidence*, pp. 145-146.

5 There are a number of fundamental concepts of evidence. To be received and considered by a court, evidence must be *material, relevant,* and *admissable.*[2] (It should be noted that the legal use of the term "material" is quite different from its use in accounting and auditing).

6 Evidence is *material* if it is offered to prove or disprove a fact in issue.[3] It is immaterial if it is a matter not requiring to be proved. In other words, something is material if it offers proof about a fact.

7 Evidence is *relevant* if it is logically capable of offering proof. Relevance requires that there must be a probative (i.e. affording proof, evidential) connection between the fact offered as evidence and the fact at issue. Relevance is the first condition of admissability. Relevance in law requires no higher degree of probability than would be required for ordinary reasoning.

8 To be *admissable*, evidence must be material, relevant and not excluded by any rule of the law of evidence (rules which arise from interpretations of federal and provincial Acts dealing with evidence and from common law). "...in the law, a jury is carefully protected from being exposed to evidence deemed unfit for their attention. ...Legal reasoning is accordingly centred around the examination of evidence. This evidence is carefully filtered, so that the jury receives only that which promises a certain amount of authenticity".[4]

9 There are several other terms that are important in a consideration of legal evidence concepts.[5]

- *Inference* — Whenever one fact is presented to prove another, an inference must be drawn.
- *Circumstantial evidence* — If more than one inference can be drawn from the evidence, then the evidence is circumstantial. If only one inference can be drawn, it is direct evidence.
- *Hearsay evidence* — This is testimony by a witness on a statement made to the witness about a relevant event or circumstance. This evidence is generally not admissable. However, an exception to this rule is testimony by an expert witness.
- *Burden of proof* — The duty to establish a case or to establish the facts upon a particular issue. This is a fundamental feature of the adversary court system — in every case, a *prima facie* case must be presented by the prosecution or the plaintiff.
- *Prima facie* — At first sight, on the first impression. An allegation which, without further evidence to the contrary, will or ought to be found true. Prima facie truth is a presumption of the truth.

---

2 *Ibid.*, p. 149.

3 *Ibid.*, p. 150.

4 Toulmin, Rieke and Janik, *An Introduction to Reasoning*, Legal Reasoning, p. 301.

5 The definitions and explanations presented have been drawn primarily from the following sources: Canadian Encyclopedic Digest (Western Edition), Vol II Title 57, *Evidence*; Delisle, R. J., *Evidence Principles and Problems*, Second Edition, Carswell,1989; Cudmore,G. D., *Civil Evidence Handbook*, Carswell, 1987; and Buzzard, J. H., May, R., Howard, M.N., *Phipson on Evidence*, Thirteenth Edition, Sweet & Maxwell,1982.

- *Standard of proof* — The degree to which proof must be established. In criminal cases, the prosecution must prove the case "beyond reasonable doubt". The standard of proof required if the prosecution is to discharge its initial evidential burden successfully is that it must have raised a case to answer, or established a *prima facie* case against the accused. In a civil case, the standard of proof required is "proof on the balance of probabilities".
- *Beyond reasonable doubt* — This has been defined in common law as "that quality and kind of doubt which, when you are dealing with matters of importance in your own affairs, you allow to influence you one way or another". It is described as "less than certainty".
- *Balance of probabilities* — This has been defined in law as: "If it is more probable than not, that is sufficient proof. If the probability of two allegations being correct is equal, it is not sufficient".
- *Weight of evidence* — Primarily related to the sufficiency of evidence, but also affected by the relevance and reliability of the evidence. Used in the same way as degree of proof. In law, it is impossible to lay down in words any scale or standard by which you can measure the degree of proof which will suffice to support a particular conclusion of fact.
- *Preponderance of evidence* — The evidence with the most weight; the standard of proof used in most civil cases. It refers to the proof that leads the trier of fact to find that the existence of the fact in issue is more probable than not. The general rule in civil cases is that the party having the burden of proof must produce a preponderance of evidence or that such evidence (when weighed with that opposed to it) has more convincing force, from which results the greater probability in favour of the party upon whom the burden rests.

PROFESSIONAL JUDGMENT IN FINANCIAL REPORTING

Chapter 12 of the research study on professional judgment in financial reporting 10
provides a summary of findings on the nature of professional judgment.[6] These findings (except for those dealing with specific aspects of financial reporting) are:

1. Professional judgment implies a meaningful choice (otherwise the decision would be self-evident or trivial). In the financial reporting arena, such judgment involves difficult and complex issues and consequences that are significant to those concerned. Part of what makes the choice meaningful is that it is likely to be carried out under substantial uncertainty about at least some components of the problem, perhaps including consequences of some potential courses of action.

2. The professional judgment process is complex and subtle: simplistic analysis or views of it are not helpful. Prior research indicated this, as did the analyses of responses to the professional judgment cases (including the comments many respondents made about complexities) and the review of complex issues in the preceding chapter.

3. The exercise of professional judgment is central to what it means to be a professional. Therefore professional due care, objectivity and integrity are essential to the process.

---

[6] Gibbins, Michael and Mason, Alister K., *Professional Judgment in Financial Reporting*, CICA 1988.

4. Professional judgment is a process that takes time. With experience and expertise, this time may be shortened because memory can suggest potential solutions quickly. Some expert people are able to do this very quickly indeed. Error can occur if solutions are adopted without due care (for example, prematurely or because of perceptual biases).
5. A number of human strengths and weaknesses may affect a particular professional judgment. Therefore, memory, learning, cognition and other mental processes of individuals play a significant part in the overall professional judgment process.
6. Professional judgment in financial reporting is exercised within an environment that provides motivations, constraints, costs, benefits, risks, and other (often changing) factors important to the way the professional judgment process works and to the position of the person(s) exercising such judgment.
7. Professional judgment is a continuing process. Professionals, by virtue of their knowledge and experience, are prepared to cope with problems as they arise, and the decision or consequences of one judgment may well be part of a subsequent judgment problem (as a constraint or precedent or even as an unsolved issue if not dealt with satisfactorily at first).
8. Both the nature of the professional judgment process and the quality of the result are powerfully dependent on the specifics of the particular judgment problem at hand. Professional judgment in financial reporting (like the more extensively-studied judgment in auditing) is analytical and information-based and commonly involves a number of information processing activities, including collection and evaluation of information, problem definition, analysis of alternatives, assessment of likely consequences, documentation and allied activities. Prudence, ability to justify recommendations and acceptance of personal responsibility for consequences are expected of those exercising such judgement.
9. Professional judgment in financial reporting is largely a group process; it is usually carried out within an organization or firm and several people are likely to be involved. Prior research indicates that group judgments are likely to be superior to judgments by isolated individuals, suggesting that consultation will generally improve the quality of professional judgment. The questionnaire respondents indicated that other persons were customarily involved in financial reporting judgments, and identified consultation as a prime requirement established by their organizations for dealing with judgment problems.[7]

11 The study comments on attempts that have been made to develop a probabilistic framework for use in evaluating choices. It concludes that:

> Rational decision-making models based on simple economic and probabilistic principles are not very useful in describing the professional judgment process: relative to such models, "real" professional judgment is more complex and less static, being responsive (for better or for worse) to a host of situational and other factors that are continuously changing and are difficult to incorporate in such models, and yet at the

[7] *Ibid.*, pp. 129-130.

same time is subject to various "good enough" rules of thumb, practical "good sense" and other simplifications that are at variance with logically complete decision making.[8]

LOGIC AND REASONING

Questions have been raised by Stephen Toulmin and Jonathan Cohen, among others, regarding the inappropriate use of "scientific" logic concepts. They have questioned attempts to apply principles of logic based on mathematical probability to fields where reasoning processes are complex and reaching conclusions is not necessarily a logical, sequential, rational process. Toulmin, for example, observed that: 12

> ...the science of logic has throughout its history tended to develop in a direction leading it away from these [everyday] issues, away from practical questions about the manner in which we have occasion to handle and criticise arguments in different fields, and towards a condition of complete autonomy, in which logic becomes a theoretical study on its own, as free from all immediate practical concerns as is some branch of pure mathematics; and even though at all stages in its history there have been people who were prepared to raise again questions about the application of logic, some of the questions vital for an understanding of this application have scarcely been raised.[9]

In the same vein, Cohen is concerned with the inappropriate application of "the mathematicist theory". He notes, for instance that: 13

> ...in everyday life we very often have to form beliefs about individual matters of fact in a context of incomplete information. We need something better then than a concept of probability which is conclusively applicable to our inferences only on the assumption that we already have all the relevant premisses. What may well serve our purposes instead is a concept that not only tells us which conclusion is favoured by the evidence we do have, but also grades how extensive a coverage of the relevant issues is achieved by this evidence.[10]

Cohen also notes that: 14

> ...there is one field of discussion where an everyday [as opposed to a mathematicist] concept of probability is undeniably used within a fairly determinate framework — in British, Australasian and North American courts of law[11].
>
> ...if the mathematicist theory does not fit the mode of reasoning that is proper for lay juries, and jurymen are supposed to carry the principles of their everyday reasonings into the jury-room, the mathematicist theory must be wrong for much of everyday discourse also.[12]

Toulmin reaches somewhat similar conclusions: 15

> Logic is concerned with the soundness of the claims we make — with the solidity of the grounds we produce to support them, the firmness of the backing we provide for them — or, to change the metaphor, with the sort of *case* we present in defence of our claims. The legal analogy implied in this last way of putting the point can for once be

---

8 *Ibid.*, pp. 26-27.

9 Toulmin, Stephen, *The Uses of Argument*, Cambridge University Press, 1958, p. 2.

10 Cohen, L. Jonathan, *The Probable and the Provable*, Oxford University Press, 1977, p. 39.

11 *Ibid.*, p. 43.

12 *Ibid.*, p. 44.

a real help. So let us forget about psychology, sociology, technology and mathematics, ignore the echoes of structural engineering and *collage* in the words "grounds" and "backing", and take as our model the discipline of jurisprudence. Logic (we may say) is generalised jurisprudence. Arguments can be compared with lawsuits..., while the cases we present in making good each kind of claim can be compared with each other.[13]

There is one special virtue in the parallel between logic and jurisprudence: it helps to keep in the centre of the picture the *critical* function of the reason. The rules of logic may not be tips or generalisations: they none the less apply to men and their arguments — not in the way that laws of psychology or maxims of method apply, but rather as *standards of achievement* which a man, in arguing, can come up to or fall short of, and by which his arguments can be judged. A sound argument, a well-grounded or firmly-backed claim, is one which will stand up to criticism, one for which a case can be presented coming up to the standard required if it is to deserve a favourable verdict.[14]

---

[13] Toulmin, p. 7.

[14] *Ibid.*, p. 8.

Appendix F

SUMMARY OF SURVEY QUESTIONNAIRE RESPONSES

RESULTS OF A SURVEY OF CURRENT PRACTICE

This appendix provides a summary of the results obtained by mailing a questionnaire on VFM audit evidence to 75 practitioners, including federal, provincial and municipal auditors, representatives from public accounting firms and internal auditors. Those who received the questionnaire included both senior officials and those directly involved in conducting VFM audits. 1

A summary of those responding in each category is as follows: 2

* Provincial	19
Federal	10
Municipal	4
CA firms	7
Internal audit	2
	42

* Responses were received from all of the provinces with value-for-money mandates.

The questionnaire was designed with two main purposes in mind: 3

- To obtain views on current practice so that similarities and differences could be identified and discussed in the study.
- To get the opinions of practitioners on desirable and undesirable practices related to obtaining and evaluating VFM evidence.

The questionnaires were sent out at an early stage of this project, before evidence concepts and conclusions had been formulated by the Study Group. The questionnaire covers a broad range of issues rather than concentrating on those concepts and issues that eventually proved to be of most interest to the Study Group. 4

ANALYSIS OF RESPONSES

5 The following summary shows the responses to each of the questions in the questionnaire (reference should be made to Appendix B for the exact wording of the questions; many of the questions in the response summary have been abbreviated to improve the readability of the analysis). For some questions, the order of parts of the question have been changed to reflect the degree of support received.

6 Responses to Question 15, *Reaction to Statements about VFM Audit Evidence*, have been shown as percentages rather than as the actual number of responses. This converts the responses to a common unit of measurement, since many respondents did not answer all of the questions; for example, five responses marked as "strongly agree" to one question are not necessarily equivalent to five similar responses to another question. A brief statement has been added to each of the 26 parts of this question which tries to reflect the messages that the responses appear to convey.

7 Responses to Question 17 on *Evidence Requirements in Specific Situations* have been summarized by the support given to various types of supporting evidence required for each assertion. Some respondents listed only one type of evidence, others several. In addition, some latitude has been taken in grouping similar responses, since different language is used to describe the nature of the evidence to be obtained.

8 Finally, the questionnaire contained many specific comments and examples for each question. Many of these comments have been used to interpret and assess the results of the survey. They have provided valuable insights into present practices and form a key element in the study's conclusions on VFM audit evidence.

NATURE AND EXTENT OF THE EVIDENCE

	RATING					PRIORITY		
	5	4	3	2	1	1	2	3
1&2 Importance of the following in determining the nature and extent of evidence: (ranked in order of support)								
• significance of the finding (a)	29	9	3	0	1	26	4	6
• degree of certainty expressed by the audit conclusion (f)	21	16	4	0	1	3	13	9
• form of report or nature of audit assurance given (g)	15	12	9	2	3	8	4	6
• risk of the auditee's failure to meet the audit criteria (e)	8	12	13	6	3	1	5	7
• current environment in which the auditee operates (c)	6	9	22	1	2	0	5	6
• effectiveness of internal control (b)	5	11	18	7	1	2	3	3
• cost of obtaining evidence (h)	5	14	14	7	2	1	3	3
• cooperativeness of auditee and receptiveness to audit (d)	4	8	10	14	4	1	3	0
• time constraints (i)	4	8	15	9	5	0	2	2

		YES	NO	MAYBE
3.	**Must evidence be gathered for each of the following?** (ranked in order of support)			
	• assertion of fact	40	2	
	• conclusions or opinions	37	3	1
	• audit criteria	33	7	
	• recommendations	25	16	1
	• management's responses	13	26	

		YES	NO
4.	**To whom must the sufficiency and appropriateness of evidence be demonstrated?** (ranked in order of support)		
	• the auditee organization	32	10
	• an advisory committee	28	12
	• an Office quality control function	25	13
	• members of Office not involved in the audit	24	17
	• only yourself	2	39

		YES	NO
5.	**Does the reliability of evidence vary with the source?**	39	3

		RATING					PRIORITY		
		5	4	3	2	1	1	2	3
6&7	**Techniques used to obtain evidence:** (ranked in order of support)								
	• oral enquiry of persons inside the organization being audited (e)	37	4	1	0	0	14	11	7
	• inspection of records or documents (a)	32	9	0	1	0	12	11	3
	• observation and documentation of processes or procedures (d)	23	13	3	3	0	4	8	3
	• analysis of components and interrelationships contained in financial and other information (j)	16	19	7	0	0	3	0	5
	• visits to work sites (c)	19	18	4	1	0	1	1	4
	• comparison of auditee with other similar organizations (k)	11	19	8	3	1	0	3	5

	RATING					PRIORITY		
	5	4	3	2	1	1	2	3
• analysis and evaluation of the system of internal control (l)	13	8	9	9	3	0	2	3
• reliance on the work of a specialist (n)	7	16	4	10	5	1	0	4
• oral enquiry of persons outside the organization being audited (g)	7	8	16	9	2	0	1	3
• checking the arithmetic accuracy of data provided by the auditee or performing independent calculations (i)	8	15	14	3	2	1	1	2
• written enqiry or confirmation addressed to persons inside the organization being audited (f)	5	6	16	13	2	2	1	0
• inspection of physical assets (b)	5	13	14	8	2	0	0	0
• reliance on internal audit or program evaluation (m)	5	6	13	10	6	1	0	0
• written enquiry or confirmation addressed to persons outside the organization being audited (h)	3	5	12	15	7	0	0	0

		YES	NO
8.	**Before obtaining evidence, do you define the characteristics that indicate when an audit criterion has been met?**	39	1

9. **Are audit criteria supported by evidence in the same sense that audit findings and conclusions are supported? If required, what kind of evidence would normally be needed?** (only narrative answers were requested)

		OFFICE POLICIES	PERSONAL JUDGMENT
10.	**Is the nature and extent of evidence gathered governed by Office policies or personal judgment?**	7	28

		FREQUENCY				
		1	2	3	4	5
11.	**Indicate the frequency of using sampling techniques —** from Rarely (1) to Very Frequently (5):					
a)	**statistical sampling**	8	14	12	6	1
b)	**judgmental sampling**	1	2	9	18	12

		YES	NO
12.	**Are the concepts of "reliance on internal control" and "compliance testing" relevant to value-for-money auditing?**	28	9

		YES	NO
13.			
a)	**Do you evaluate the effectiveness of internal control for all major systems?**	12	16
b)	**Do you evaluate the overall system of internal control rather than controls in each separate system?**	20	6

		YES	NO
14.	**When using statistical data obtained internally, do you test its reliability?**	27	6

		RANGE				
		1	2	3	4	5
15.	**REACTION TO STATEMENTS ABOUT VFM AUDIT EVIDENCE** **Extent of agreement or disagreement with 26 statements about VFM audit evidence:** (percentage range from strongly agree to strongly disagree) (percentage who agree, are neutral and disagree are in brackets)					
a)	Evidence for positive finding is much more important than for a negative one.	5	3	22	22	48
	(Generally disagree)	(8)		(22)	(70)	
b)	No more evidence is needed if auditee agrees to finding.	16	32	10	16	26
	(Split — more agree, but many strongly disagree)	(48)		(10)	(42)	
c)	Statements in interviews are not evidence, but may lead to other sources of evidence.	25	25	20	25	5
	(Split, but majority agree)	(50)		(20)	(30)	
d)	In a disagreement between experts, I favour mine.	6	17	47	11	19
	(Undecided, but tend to disagree)	(23)		(47)	(30)	
e)	I usually accept an internal audit report or consultant's report as supporting evidence.	28	39	18	10	5
	(Generally agree)	(67)		(18)	(15)	
f)	It's very difficult to gather evidence that systems are not in place or that something does not exist.	18	15	15	32	20
	(Split, but tend to disagree)	(33)		(15)	(52)	
g)	There is less rigour in evidence for "soft" issues than for "hard" ones.	24	46	14	8	8
	(Generally agree)	(70)		(14)	(16)	
h)	It's preferable to have very strong evidence, but I will report important findings based on relatively weak evidence.	18	39	18	10	15
	(Majority agree, but minority strongly disagree)	(57)		(18)	(25)	
i)	For very sensitive issues, the evidence must be absolutely convincing.	30	35	22	10	3
	(Generally agree)	(65)		(22)	(13)	
j)	Sometimes a piece of evidence is so convincing I don't need any other corroboration.	36	32	22	7	3
	(Generally agree)	(68)		(22)	(10)	

		RANGE				
		1	2	3	4	5
k)	I don't require as much evidence when reporting on specific deficiencies.	15	26	7	26	26
	(Split, but tend to disagree)	(41)		(7)	(52)	
l)	When giving an overall opinion, I need evidence for facts in the report, but not for the opinion.	0	14	11	0	75
	(Strongly disagree)	(14)		(11)	(75)	
m)	If my report will receive unusual attention, I require very convincing evidence.	26	44	15	10	5
	(Generally agree)	(70)		(15)	(15)	
n)	Two or more oral representations are acceptable if they corroborate one another.	12	45	25	13	5
	(Generally agree)	(57)		(25)	(18)	
o)	I plan to gather evidence that will lead to a correct evaluation, regardless of prior expectations.	58	17	3	14	8
	(Strongly agree)	(75)		(3)	(22)	
p)	For system deficiencies, I don't insist on seeing evidence that a problem has occurred.	8	12	25	20	35
	(Generally disagree)	(20)		(25)	(55)	
q)	In some areas, I can't expect to convince everyone, so I don't go after really strong evidence.	8	17	25	25	25
	(Generally disagree)	(25)		(25)	(50)	
r)	I always have some supporting evidence, even for relatively minor items in the report.	55	26	16	0	3
	(Strongly agree)	(81)		(16)	(3)	
s)	If the auditee agrees with the criteria, I don't require further support.	18	33	13	10	26
	(Majority agree, but minority strongly disagree)	(51)		(13)	(36)	
t)	For recommendations, I must have supporting evidence.	39	20	20	18	3
	(Generally agree)	(59)		(20)	(21)	
u)	Even if the evidence is not strong, the more evidence I get, the more comfortable I feel.	35	38	15	10	2
	(Generally agree)	(73)		(15)	(12)	
v)	An opinion of an outside expert is the best evidence.	5	12	33	25	25
	(Generally disagree)	(17)		(33)	(50)	

		RANGE				
		1	2	3	4	5
w)	Copies are as good as the original documents.	5	20	25	35	15
	(Split, but majority disagree)	(25)		(25)	(50)	
x)	Written confirmation of statements made in interviews is not required.	32	23	25	17	3
	(Generally agree)	(55)		(25)	(20)	
y)	I don't need evidence to support decisions on scope and objectives, just for the contents of the final report.	10	5	15	26	44
	(Strongly disagree)	(15)		(15)	(70)	
z)	It's impossible to give other than very general guidance about the nature and extent of evidence needed.	19	39	26	13	3
	(Generally agree)	(58)		(26)	(16)	

16. EVIDENCE REQUIREMENTS IN SPECIFIC SITUATIONS

(Evidence required to support the following assertions — the number of respondents who mentioned one or more of the following is shown in brackets):

a) Most job descriptions are outdated.

- oral enquiry and statistical sample (5)
- judgmental sample (8)
- sampling (5)
- oral or interview evidence (7)
- inspection of documents (6)
- compare to actual performance (7)
- statement from management that descriptions are outdated (3)
- compare to other organizations (2)
- document procedures and statistical sample (2)
- reliance on expert (1)
- evidence on non-conformity (deficiency) (1)
- written enquiry (1)

Several questioned the usefulness of job descriptions, and considered the assertion irrelevant.

b) No procedures exist to ensure that money is advanced to recipient organizations only as and when needed.

- observation of process (4)
- document systems and procedures (6)

- inspect records and documents (111)
- judgmental sample (4)
- statistical sample (3)
- determine consequences (4)
- sampling (3)
- visit recipient organization (2)
- interviews — inside and outside the organization (3)
- written enquiry outside the organization (1)
- use of contribution audit expertise (1)
- comparison with other agencies (1)

c) Reports do not contain appropriate measures of past performance.

- analysis and evaluation (5)
- oral enquiry (4)
- interviews (3)
- sampling (1)
- compare reported performance with standards in use (6)
- review reports (6)
- document procedures (1)
- review procedures (1)
- compare with similar entity (1)

d) The planned cost of a major capital project was $10 million; benefits were projected at $7 million; the actual cost was $12 million.

- inspection of documents (13)
- analysis and evaluation (7)
- oral enquiries inside the organization (4)
- review process and procedures (3)
- test accounting records (4)
- obtain expert advice (4)
- review cost systems (3)
- interviews (3)
- judgmental sample (1)
- oral enquiries outside the organization (2)
- written confirmation of costs (2)
- experience with similar projects (1)

e) The operation of the claim verification unit in the department is carried out efficiently.

- review work of internal auditors (18)
- test check work of internal auditors (7)
- compare with other similar operations (2)
- compare to accepted standards (4)
- use a productivity expert (3)

- assess capability of internal auditors (3)
- document systems (1)
- interview staff (1)
- check arithmetic accuracy (1)
- review external constraints (1)

f) Management has formulated a plan to address deficiencies in the accounts receivable system and the plan is being implemented. Management's actions should rectify the problem.

- review and document plan (9)
- analyze and assess action taken (9)
- review adequacy of plan (3)
- interview management (4)
- compare progress with planned action (3)
- confirm plan and action taken (2)
- oral enquiry outside the organization (2)
- testing (1)
- observation and documentation of procedures (1)
- review budgets to assess whether resources are allocated (1)

	YES	NO
17. FURTHER RESEARCH AND GUIDANCE **Have you encountered situations where you would have liked more authoritative guidance on the nature and extent of evidence required?**	9	26

BIBLIOGRAPHY

A *Framework for the Conduct of Special Examinations in Crown Corporations*, Office of the Auditor General of Canada, 1987

A *Statement of Basic Auditing Concepts*, American Accounting Association, Studies in Accounting Research #6, 1973

AICPA *Statement on Auditing Standards*, Codification of Auditing Standards and Procedures No. 1, 1973.

An Approach to Comprehensive Auditing, A Paper by the Office of the Auditor General of Canada, September 1981

Anderson, R.J., *The External Audit*, Second Edition, Copp Clark Pitman, 1984

Ashton, R.H., *Research in Audit Decision Making: Rationale, Evidence, and Implications*, Canadian CGA Research Foundation, 1983

Canadian Encyclopedic Digest (Western Edition) Vol. II, Title 57, Evidence, Thomson Professional Publishing Canada, August, 1988

Cohen, L. Jonathan, *The Probable and the Provable*, Oxford University Press, 1977

Copi, Irving M., *Introduction to Logic*, Fifth Edition, Macmillan Publishing Co., 1978

Comprehensive Auditing — Concepts, Components and Characteristics, Canadian Comprehensive Auditing Foundation

Comprehensive Auditing Manual, Office of the Auditor General of Canada, 1990

Cudmore, G.D., *Civil Evidence Handbook*, Carswell, 1987

Cutt, J., *Comprehensive Auditing in Canada*, Theory and Practice, Praeger,1988

Davis, D.F., Do You Want a Performance Audit or a Program Evaluation?, *Public Administration Review*, pp. 35-41, Jan/Feb 1990

Deslisle, R.J., *Evidence Principles and Problems*, Second Edition, Carswell, 1989

Estey, The Honourable W.Z., *Report of the Inquiry into the Collapse of the CCB and Northland Bank*, August 1986

Evidence in Comprehensive Auditing, Canadian Comprehensive Auditing Foundation Professional Development Course,

Extent of Audit Testing, (Toronto: CICA, 1980)

Gaa, J.C., Discussion of A theory of evidence based on audit assertions, *Contemporary Accounting Research* Vol. 6, No 2, pp. 427-431, 1990

Gibbins, M. and Mason, A.K., *Professional Judgment in Financial Reporting*, (Toronto: CICA, 1988)

Gibbs, T.E., A general theory of evidence as the conceptual foundation in auditing theory: a comment, *The Accounting Review*, pp 751-755, July 1977

Guide on the Program Evaluation Function, Office of the Comptroller of Canada, May 1981

International Organization of Supreme Audit Institutions, INTOSAI *Auditing Standards*, June 1989

Keenan, Joy, VFM audits get some guidance, *CA Magazine*, April, 1990, pp. 25-26.

Kissinger, J.N., A general theory of evidence as the conceptual foundation in auditing theory - some comments and extensions, *The Accounting Review*, pp. 322-339, April, 1977

Leslie, D.A., *Materiality, The Concept and its Application to Auditing*, (Toronto: CICA, 1985)

Mautz, R.K. and Sharaf, H.A., *The Philosophy of Auditing*, American Accounting Association, Monograph No. 6, 1961

Parker, L.D., *Value-for-Money Auditing: Conceptual, Development and Operational Issues*, Australian Accounting Research Foundation, Auditing Discussion Paper No. 1, 1986

Phipson on Evidence, Thirteenth Edition, Buzzard, J.H., May, R., and Howard, M.N., Sweet and Maxwell, 1982

Reporting and Auditing Effectiveness, The Experience of Canada Mortgage and Housing Corporation, CCAF Applied Research Series, 1990

Smieliauskas, W. and Smith, L., A theory of evidence based on audit assertions, *Contemporary Accounting Research* Vol. 6 No. 2, pp. 407-426, 1990

Stephens, R.G., An Investigation of the Descriptiveness of the General Theory of Evidence and Auditing, *Auditing: A Journal of Practice & Theory*, Vol. 3 No. 1, Fall 1983

Swedish National Audit Bureau, *System-Oriented Effectiveness Audit - Concept & Implementation*, 1985

Toba, Y., A general theory of evidence as the conceptual foundation in auditing theory, *The Accounting Review*, pp. 7-24, January 1975

Toba, Y,. A reply, *The Accounting Review*, pp. 756-758, July 1977

Toulmin, S., Rieke, R., and Janik, A., *An Introduction to Reasoning*, Second Edition, McMillan Publishing Company, 1984

Toulmin, S., *The Uses of Argument*, Cambridge University Press, 1958

United States General Accounting Office, *Government Auditing Standards*, 1988 Revision

Zelman, M., *Evidence in Value-for-Money Auditing*, Discussion Paper No. 2, Office of the Auditor General of Canada, January, 1980